U2

BANDS THAT ROCK!

Angie Timmons

Enslow Publishing
101 W. 23rd Street
Suite 240
New York, NY 10011
USA

enslow.com

Published in 2019 by Enslow Publishing, LLC.

101 W. 23rd Street, Suite 240, New York, NY 10011

Copyright © 2019 by Enslow Publishing, LLC

Library of Congress Cataloging-in-Publication Data

Names: Timmons, Angie, author.
Title: U2 / Angie Timmons.
Description: New York : Enslow Publishing, 2019. | Series: Bands that rock! | Audience: Grades 7-12 |
Includes bibliographical references and index.
Identifiers: LCCN 2018012869| ISBN 9781978503540 (library bound) | ISBN 9781978505292 (pbk.)
Subjects: LCSH: U2 (Musical group)—Juvenile literature. | Rock musicians—Ireland—Biography—Juvenile literature.
Classification: LCC ML3930.U2 T56 2019 | DDC 782.42166092/2—dc23
LC record available at https://lccn.loc.gov/2018012869

Printed in China

To Our Readers: We have done our best to make sure all website addresses in book were active and appropriate when we went to press. However, the author and publisher have no control over and assume no liability for the material available those websites or on any websites they may link to. Any comments or suggestions be sent by email to customerservice@enslow.com.

Photo Credits: Cover, p. 1 Jeff Kravitz/FilmMagic/Getty Images (Bono); cover, p. 1 Steve Mack/FilmMagic/Getty Images (U2); pp. 4, 70 Paul Bergen/Redferns/Getty Images; p. 6 Alex Bowie/Hulton Archive/Getty Images; pp. 9, 20 Photoshot/Hulton Archive/Getty Images; pp. 14, 17 Virginia Turbett/Redferns/Getty Images; p. 23 Pe Noble/Redferns/Getty Images; p. 28 Martyn Goddard/Corbis Historical/Getty Imag p. 30 Peter Albrektsen/Shutterstock.com; p. 31 TheCoverVersion/Alamy Stock Ph p. 35 ullstein bild/Getty Images; pp. 36–37 Larry Hulst/Michael Ochs Archives/ Getty Images; p. 41 AFP/Getty Images; pp. 42–43 Richard E. Aaron/Redferns/Gett Images; p. 45 Independent News and Media/Hulton Archive/Getty Images; pp. 48– Peter Carrette Archive/Hulton Archive/Getty Images; pp. 50, 66 Peter Still/Redfer Getty Images; p. 55 Sputnik Aloysius/Shutterstock.com; p. 58 Everett Collection; 61 Gysembergh Benoit/Paris Match Archive/Getty Images; pp. 64–65 Anna Krajec Michael Ochs Archives/Getty Images; p. 73 Junko Kimura/Getty Images; p. 76 Jed Jacobsohn/Getty Images; pp. 78–79 Evan Agostini/Getty Images; p. 80 US Coast Guard/Getty Images; pp. 83, 86, 89 Kevin Mazur/WireImage/Getty Images; p. 90 Robin Marchant/WireImage/Getty Images; cover and interior pages Macrovector/ Shutterstock.com (guitar illustration); Jemastock/Shutterstock.com (hand icon).

CONTENTS

Still together after all these years, original U2 members (*from left*) Larry Mullen, Adam Clayton, the Edge, and Bono arrive at Schipol Airport in the Netherlands in 2001.

Introduction

"**T**hree years after Omagh, let's turn this song into a prayer . . . I'm so sick of it! We've had enough!"

These were the words U2's front man, Bono, inserted into the band's 2001 performance of their iconic song "Sunday Bloody Sunday" at Ireland's Slane Castle, almost twenty years after the song appeared on the band's third album, *War*. The band's original recording of the song all those years ago was inspired by an alarming uptick in violence between religious and political factions in the band's home country of Ireland. Its original lyrics, repeated by Bono at Slane in 2001, beseeched listeners to consider when the violence would finally end: "How long must we sing this song?"[1]

For too long, as it turned out. The 1998 Omagh bombing, carried out by the Real Irish Republican Army, injured more than two hundred people and killed twenty-nine.[2] Bono ended the 2001 Slane performance by naming all twenty-nine people killed in the bombing.

"Sunday Bloody Sunday" encapsulates U2's blend of evocative sound with politics, though the band has taken care to take only one side in political struggles: the side of peace, as one music writer put it:

Like many of U2's songs, "Sunday Bloody Sunday" has evolved and changed throughout the years it's been played live. When U2 performed the song on the *War* Tour, there was some trepidation on how the crowd would react, especially their Irish fans. There were some who saw the song as a glorification of the Troubles and a call for revolution. In order to squash these ideas, Bono introduced the song by saying, "This song is not a rebel song. This song is Sunday Bloody Sunday." This statement, combined with the white flags that waved behind the band on stage, helped bring forth the song's non-partisan intention for a peaceful solution.[3]

The Provisional Irish Republican Army carried out bombings in Belfast, Northern Ireland, on April 14, 1972.

The song references an actual incident known as Bloody Sunday: on January 30, 1972, a demonstration by Catholic civil rights supporters in the Northern Ireland town of Londonderry turned deadly when British paratroopers fired on the peaceful demonstrators, ultimately killing fourteen and injuring thirteen others.[4] The song has become an anthem for the band to call attention to humanitarian violations and other causes Bono and the band's members have taken up in their more than forty years as a group. Though the Irish civil strife that originally inspired the song has subsided in the last twenty years, "Sunday Bloody Sunday" remains emblematic of the sociopolitical direction the band has steadily been going in for forty years. The band has consistently used its profile to draw attention to global crises, such as poverty, famine, AIDS, and violence, and its members have been responsible for some of the most significant celebrity acts of charity in modern history.

While attempting to save the world, U2 has also been a high-achieving musical force. In its more than four decades in existence, U2 has sold more than 170 million records worldwide and won dozens of awards, from Grammy Awards to American Music Awards, MTV Video Music Awards, Q Awards, Juno Awards, NME Awards, and Golden Globes. They're the twenty-first-highest-selling music artist in the United States and have achieved similar status in Europe and the United Kingdom. On *Rolling Stone*'s list of the 100 Greatest Artists of All Time, U2 ranks high at number twenty-two. In 2005, in the band's first year of eligibility, U2 was inducted into the Rock and Roll Hall of Fame.[5]

Formed in Dublin amid a turbulent 1970s' Ireland, U2's members were mere teenagers at the band's inception. They've grown up together, in long-standing friendships and a higher purpose: to change the world.

From Schoolmates to Bandmates

In the fall of 1976, a fourteen-year-old student and budding drummer named Larry Mullen Jr. posted an advertisement on a bulletin board at his school, Mount Temple Comprehensive School in Dublin: "Drummer Seeks Musicians to Form Band."[1]

On September 25, 1976, six of Larry's schoolmates showed up at his house in response to the advertisement he'd posted at school. On that day, in the Mullen family kitchen, a band was formed by Larry, a drummer; Adam Clayton, a bassist; Paul Hewson, a musician/vocalist who would later be known as "Bono"; Dave Evans, a guitarist who later became known as "The Edge" or just "Edge"; Dave's older brother, Richard "Dick" Evans, who also played the guitar; and Mullen's friends Ivan McCormick and Peter Martin. The band formed under the name Larry Mullen Band.

McCormick and Martin soon left the band, and within two years, Dick Evans parted ways with the group.

The foursome that remained—Larry, Paul (Bono), Dave (Edge), and Adam—became U2.

The young men of U2, (*from left*) Bono, Larry Mullen Jr., Adam Clayton, and the Edge, pose for a group shot in the early 1980s.

From Schoolmates to Bandmates

Little did they know the ragtag group that formed in Larry's kitchen would go on to become one of the biggest bands of all time.

Trouble in Ireland

At the time of U2's formation, its members were just teenagers; in fact, as the band grew, its youngest and founding member, Larry, was often restricted by curfews set and enforced by his parents. Though many prominent bands have been formed by teenagers seeking to express themselves, rebel, or become rich and famous, U2's young members faced more hurdles than just their youth.

Dublin in the 1970s was a largely working-class city that, in many ways, embodied Ireland's long struggles with poverty and self-governance. Few resources to form and succeed as a band existed: "Ireland was a cultural backwater that drowned anyone who stayed for too long. It was against this hopeless backdrop that a fourteen-year-old boy called Larry Mullen pinned a note on the bulletin board."[2]

Dave and Adam came from reasonably comfortable middle-class families who had relocated to Dublin from England for professional reasons; their families lived in Malahide, an affluent suburb north of Dublin. The band's two native sons, Paul and Larry, also hailed from middle-class families, but they lived in more working-class suburbs closer to Dublin's center and had different childhood experiences; for instance, while Adam was sent to pricey English-style boarding schools, Paul grew up in a rough north Dublin neighborhood that in many ways inspired his passionate, take-charge personality and his eventual activism for efforts such as global debt relief. His family lived on a street that served as the dividing line between two rough neighborhoods: the Ballymun Flats—public housing high-rises, or "projects," built when Paul was a young boy to house poor people forced out of the inner city—

and West Finglas. Caught between the two neighborhoods, the man who's now known for peaceful pursuits was a violent boy who hated bullies and stood up for himself in street fights, though he never liked the violence. His distaste for violence is what attracted him to peaceful icons like Mahatma Gandhi and Martin Luther King Jr.

Larry grew up in a north Dublin suburb, Artane, that—like Paul's neighborhood—was home to public housing for Dublin's poorer residents.[3]

In addition to their varying degrees of "middle-class" backgrounds, the chances of U2's young founding members coming together were slim in Ireland in the 1970s; without Mount Temple Comprehensive School, it's unlikely all four of the bands' members—who came from different religious and national backgrounds—would have had cause to cross paths. Mount Temple was one of the first interdenominational schools in Ireland, meaning it enrolled students regardless of their religious identities, when Ireland was still torn by violent political and religious divisions known as "the Troubles," a conflict that lasted for thirty years, from 1968 to 1998.[4] The mere concept of Irish Catholics and Protestants coming together was practically unfathomable. U2's members unearthed lasting inspiration in the unity they found at school while the nation around them exploded in violence.

With two native Irish members (Larry and Paul) and two English-born members (Adam and Dave; the latter, while born in England, came from a Welsh family), U2 as a unit was unique. By default, Adam and Dave were from Protestant backgrounds, and when they were young, their families became friendly through a community of Protestant Brits that were largely out of place in Dublin, the capital of the Republic of Ireland. (Though Adam and Dave knew each other as children, they lost touch when Adam was sent to boarding schools; they reunited as teenagers at Mount

From Schoolmates to Bandmates

For eight hundred years, Ireland lived under the harsh and repressive rule of Britain. In the early twentieth century, Irish revolutionaries fought for independence, a fight that finally culminated in 1922 with the Irish Free State (renamed Ireland in 1937 and declared the Republic of Ireland in 1949). Protestant-heavy Northern Ireland remained loyal to Britain, frustrating the revolutionaries' vision of a completely free and unified Ireland, and unrest between Protestants and Catholics in Northern Ireland brewed. The unrest became violent in the 1960s, and British troops were deployed to support Northern Ireland in 1969, angering the republicans and starting the Troubles. As U2's members entered their formative years in the 1970s, Ireland erupted in violence. More than 3,500 people died before the 1998 Belfast Agreement ended the conflict. However, nationalists on both sides of the north-south border still want Northern Ireland to join the Republic of Ireland.[5]

Temple.) Larry came from a Catholic family. Paul came from a "split" household, in which his mother was a Protestant and his father a Catholic: "Their love affair was practically illicit at the time . . . The country was almost at civil war along religious lines, with a Catholic power base running this new nation while Protestantism was seen as the faith of our former masters, the invaders' religion."[6]

By sheer virtue of their backgrounds, U2's members had special insight into the factious relationship between the nations in which they were born. When the band formed, the Troubles still raged, providing inspiration for the band's politically and socially rich lyrics and music, as Larry summarizes: "We all have views on what our Irishness means to us . . . U2 are a living example of the kind of unity of faith and tradition that is possible in Northern Ireland."[7]

The Boys in the Band

Despite the obstacles posed by the era in which its members came of age, U2 has remained together for more than forty years, making headlines for their many record-setting achievements, political and social stances, and the philanthropic work of its members. But who are the men behind the powerhouse band?

Lawrence "Larry" Mullen Jr. (Drummer)

Born October 31, 1961, in Dublin, Larry is U2's drummer and the father of the band. After all, it was his advertisement posted on a bulletin board at school that brought its members together in the first place. Larry's musical education began early: at age eight, Larry began attending a music school, learning to play the piano. At age ten, he began drumming. For a brief time, Larry was part of a local marching band, the Artane Boys Band. His time with the marching band inspired some of his most profound contributions to U2's sound, such as the warlike drumbeats that provide the foundation for "Sunday Bloody Sunday."

Larry's interest in drumming continued. He saved up to buy his own drum kit. His parents set certain times in which he could practice his drumming at home, and he took drumming lessons from a famous Irish musician named

From Schoolmates to Bandmates

Larry Mullen Jr., shown here in 1980, is the founder and drummer of U2.

Joe Bonnie. His father, Larry Mullen Sr., was a civil servant in Dublin and got his son involved in the Post Office Workers Band, which performed a combination of orchestral and marching band music.

Like many musicians, Larry didn't grow to adulthood without his share of tragedies that pushed him toward artistic endeavors. His younger sister, Mary, died in 1973. Before her death, Larry's father had earnestly pushed his son to attend Catholic schools, he but gave up the fight after losing his youngest daughter. Instead of Catholic school, Larry landed at Mount Temple Comprehensive School, where he found his future bandmates.

Five years after Mary's death, Larry's mother, Maureen, died in a car accident. While he remained in the fledgling U2, he entertained the idea of other career paths: after leaving school, he worked for an American oil company in Dublin and considered a career in computer programming with the company's geology department. The loss of his mother, however, factored heavily into his recommitment to the band he'd formed. He left his oil company job after a year.

While Larry technically had some formal training in drumming, he wasn't a strong drummer by the time U2 formed, making his early days with the band uncertain. When the band received its first serious record deal from CBS Ireland, the record label had an uncomfortable demand: U2 had to drop Larry and find a new drummer. The other three members refused to kick out the band's founding member. CBS Ireland acquiesced, and the record deal was made. Working closely with bassist Adam Clayton to build up the band's rhythms, Larry secured his position as an integral part of U2.

Because he plays without strict adherence to traditional form but instead with spirit and instinct, Larry views his style as unique; so unique, in fact, that he has called

From Schoolmates to Bandmates

it "unteachable." He also simply wanted to "physically hit the thing,"[8] making the drums a more natural choice than the other instrument he played as a child, the piano (although he would revisit the piano much later in U2's career). Of all U2's members, Larry is the "quiet one," often preferring his bandmates to conduct interviews while he sits quietly to the side, and he's been notoriously quiet about his private life with his longtime partner, Ann Acheson, and their three children.[9] In 2016, *Rolling Stone* ranked Mullen the ninety-sixth greatest drummer of all time.[10]

Adam Clayton (Bassist)

Born March 13, 1960, in England, U2's bassist, Adam Clayton, moved to Dublin when he was five years old. His father had been a pilot with the United Kingdom's Royal Air Force and moved into civil aviation. Before the Claytons settled in Ireland, they lived in Nairobi, Kenya, while his father worked as a pilot for East African Airways. Though he was young during the family's stint in Africa, Adam has recalled that time as the happiest of his childhood. Adam was sent to an English-style boarding school in Dublin at the age of eight.

Finding it difficult to fit in at the heavily sports-oriented boarding school, Adam wanted to pursue his interest in pop music. Unfortunately, the boarding school didn't allow its students to listen to pop music, so his exposure to the popular sounds of the late 1960s and the early 1970s was limited. To pursue music in the ways he was allowed, he joined the school's "Gramphone Society," listened to classical music, and took piano lessons. During his time at boarding school, Adam managed to expand his musical knowledge through the era's popular rock operas, such as *Jesus Christ Superstar* and *Hair*, which combined various musical stylings. He tried to find anything that fell between the categories of classical and pop music to get around the school's no pop music restrictions.

At age thirteen, Adam enrolled at a secondary school, St. Columba's College, a Church of Ireland boarding school. (Unlike many of the children in Dublin, Adam's family, being English, was not Catholic, but Anglican, based on the Church of England.) At St. Columba's, Adam found friends who were fans of the biggest bands of the era, such as British bands the

U2's bassist, Adam Clayton, had an early interest in pop music and tended to be an eccentric outsider at school.

From Schoolmates to Bandmates

Who and the Beatles, and American acts such as the Grateful Dead and Carole King. Inspired by his expanded exposure to popular music, Adam bought an acoustic guitar from a secondhand store and began learning to play. He joined a band at school, playing bass guitar; his mother had purchased him the instrument when he was fourteen and made him promise he'd commit to learning how to play. Shortly after, Adam transferred from boarding school to Mount Temple Comprehensive School. He was a bit of an eccentric outsider, even at the progressive Mount Temple Comprehensive School; having spent most of his life in boarding schools, he was uncomfortable at the Dublin comprehensive school and felt he needed "props" to give him confidence. He wore an Afghan coat and mirror sunglasses and carried a flask of coffee. He gravitated toward the students who smoked cigarettes. It wasn't until the first band meeting in Larry's kitchen that Adam really associated with the likes of Larry, Bono, and Edge.

After giving up on school, Adam served as U2's unofficial manager for a couple of years, booking gigs and making connections in Dublin's music community. Despite having the right look for a rock star—meaning he pushed boundaries with his image, a trait that was highly regarded in the 1970s' punk and even pop scene—Adam wasn't entirely proficient on the bass guitar. He attempted to cover this up by using music lingo that made him appear knowledgeable of music. However, his gradual improvement kept him in the band.

Clayton's time with U2 has been, on occasion, tumultuous. As a nonreligious person, he was the odd man out when Hewson, Evans, and Mullen became deeply involved with a Christian group in the early 1980s, an involvement that made them question whether they wanted to be rock stars. The rift isolated him from his bandmates and friends, but the other three eventually reconciled their spirituality with their lives in a rock band and the members reconciled. In 1989, Clayton was arrested for possession of marijuana, and he struggled with alcoholism for a time. This was most obvious at a 1994 concert in Sydney, Australia, when Clayton was too hungover to perform. That concert remains the only live performance in which all four core band members weren't onstage together. His behavior and his notable absence onstage caused strife among the band members, who began to wonder if they would ever play live again. As a result of the trouble caused by his alcoholism, Clayton got sober.[11]

Paul Hewson, aka Bono (Lead Singer)

Undoubtedly U2's most well-known member, the band's front man was born May 10, 1960, in Dublin. Paul Hewson was born into a "split" household, and his parents agreed their first child would be Anglican and the second would be Catholic. However, Paul, the second child, usually attended Protestant Church of Ireland services with his mother and older brother, despite living in the mostly Catholic Republic of Ireland during a time when Ireland was violently split over religious and political divisions.

When Paul was just fourteen, his mother collapsed from an aneurysm at her own father's funeral and died a few days later. Seeking solace in the wake of these losses and amid the Troubles, Paul struck out to find ways to cope. He joined a surrealist street gang called Lypton Village, a group that also included Evans. The group wasn't really a gang, but rather a virtual village: a private universe with its own laws and a focus on creativity and eccentricity. Its members were known for assigning nicknames to each other. Paul's Lypton Village friends gave Paul the nickname "Bono," which would stick with him for the rest of his life.[12]

Despite having little musical experience, Bono answered Larry's advertisement for band members and showed up for the first meeting. Larry intended to lead the band, but that

Bono, pictured here in the early 1980s, is U2's energetic and passionate frontman and lead singer.

intention went out the window the moment the charismatic and intense Paul walked into his kitchen for the first meeting.[13] Bono's commitment to the band and his burgeoning political and spiritual interests were unwavering: he left school early to pursue music, and his disappointed father said he could continue to live at home but would have to leave after one year if he couldn't pay his own way.

Bono dove in.

> **"Bono" comes from *Bono Vox*, an alteration of *Bonavox*, Latin for "good voice."**

In the band's early days, their musical inabilities forced them to play easy cover songs at their live shows, although Bono was eager for them to move on to covering hard music from bands such as the Rolling Stones and the Beach Boys. Because the band lacked the skills to cover more complicated music, its members were backed against a wall. Bono's solution? They'd just have to write their own lyrics and music.

Since the band's earliest days, Bono has written almost all of U2's lyrics, which are usually socially, politically, and spiritually driven. His angst about ongoing global conflicts really showed in the band's early album *War* and later albums such as *Joshua Tree* and *Achtung Baby*.

Outside of U2, Bono has achieved fame and recognition as one of the best-known philanthropists in the world. Since the band achieved worldwide recognition in the early 1980s, Bono has used his celebrity status to spearhead new organizations that champion humanitarian relief efforts and activism that spans a wide range of causes. He has worked to fight AIDS, hunger, international debt, and conflict on a global scale, and he has received many prestigious awards for his efforts, including a knighthood in the Order of the British Empire.

Bono has a reputation as a charismatic and engaging performer, a reputation he earned early on due to his impassioned performances, use of props to make political statements during concerts, and interacting with audience members.

Dave Evans, aka Edge (Guitarist)

Born on August 8, 1961, in England, Dave Evans comes from a Welsh family. U2's iconic guitarist was raised in Ireland after his family moved there when he was a young boy. To be accepted among his peers in Ireland, Dave learned early on to speak his native Welsh only at home with his family.

As a child, Dave was a student of the guitar and piano. He often practiced with his older brother, Richard ("Dick"). On a family vacation to New York City in 1978, he bought a used but legendary guitar, a 1976 Gibson Explorer Limited Edition. This guitar would go on to be featured in countless recordings.

The two Evans brothers answered Larry's advertisement for bandmates at school and were present at the first meeting at Larry's house. Dick stayed with the band for a couple of years, while Dave stayed on and became an integral part of the band under the stage name "the Edge," which is usually shortened to "Edge."

As U2 endeavored to develop its own lyrics and music early on as a way to counteract its members' weak musical skills, Edge began to stand out as the most experimental musician in the band. He began to experiment with various guitar effects by introducing multiple musical influences. Edge introduced a 1964 VOX AC30 amplifier into U2's music in the 1980s; this, combined with his guitar, developed the guitarist's signature sound, which uses delay effects and reverb (short for reverberation, a phenomenon in which sound persists after the cause of the sound stops). On later albums, Edge became a strong proponent of introducing a variety of sounds into

U2's famous guitarist, the Edge, or simply Edge, pictured here in 1980, was born in England to a Welsh family that moved to Ireland when he was a child.

Love, Loss, Loyalty: U2's Lyrical Lore

U2 has used music to express many complex issues. Mullen and Bono used music to cope with and explore the loss of close family members. Evans's tough childhood duality—being Welsh in Ireland—contributed to the development of his musical stylings.

Ireland's political strife gave U2's members early inspiration for lyrics and music. With two born-and-raised Dubliners and two British-born members, the band came together despite the Irish-British conflict that provided the backdrop to their lives for thirty years. The band faced conflicting loyalties and anger over senseless violence.

U2 also sings about love, spirituality, and unity. Much of U2's work focuses on unity, which they have achieved as a band born in a fractured nation and which they endeavor to achieve on a global scale through music and activism.

The thematic elements of U2's music have made the band powerful and relevant for more than forty years.

Evans's "the Edge" nickname was earned due his sharp facial features and sharp mind.

U2's music, such as dance, industrial, and American roots. This was not always popular among other band members and caused significant discord around 1990. However, Edge prevailed, and he was able to continue developing U2's overall signature sound. Over the years, Edge has played keyboards, the piano, and the bass guitar in various recordings and live performances.

When Mullen, Bono, and Edge became involved with a Christian group in the early 1980s and nearly broke up U2 due to concerns over reconciling their rock-and-roll lifestyle with their faith, Edge struggled more than anyone. He was the closest to leaving the band out of all of them, but the others convinced him to stay in U2.[14]

Like Bono, Edge is heavily involved in human rights and philanthropic work, including providing replacement instruments for musicians, churches, and schools who lost their instruments in 2005's catastrophic Hurricane Katrina.

In 2011, *Rolling Stone* named Edge the thirty-eighth of the "100 Greatest Guitarists of All Time." The following year, *Spin* magazine ranked him thirteenth best guitarist of all time, and in 2015, *Rolling Stone* named Edge thirty-eighth of the "100 Greatest Guitarists."[15]

From Schoolmates to Bandmates

The Early Years

After forming in 1976, the band that would one day be known as U2 spent the next couple of years trying to develop a following and a band identity. Because Larry was responsible for forming the band, the group initially went by Larry Mullen Band.

Soon, however, they changed their name to reflect one of the few musical terms they knew: "Feedback." In music, feedback is a positive loop gain that happens when a sound loop exists between an audio input, such as a microphone or guitar, and an audio output, such as a speaker. As teenagers, the band's members knew little about music or even, in some cases, about the instruments they played. What little musical knowledge they brought to Larry's kitchen table that fateful day in 1976 was garnered from sporadic music lessons at school or through self-taught study.

Between 1976 and 1978, still struggling to find their footing and gain a following, the remaining five members changed the band's name to the Hype.[1] Finally, right before a pivotal March 1978 performance in Limerick, Ireland, they changed their name to U2. The name was suggested by a friend; the band chose it from a list of six suggestions, liking how it lent itself to open-ended

"U2" was one of six band names suggested by a friend.

interpretations—and because it was the name they least disliked from the list.[2]

Under its various names, the band began playing in small Dublin venues in 1977, and occasionally in other small venues across Ireland. They wouldn't begin playing internationally until late 1979, when they finally performed their first shows outside of Ireland. They played in London and toured across the British Isles. Before they could do that, however, they needed a big win.

The Big Break

In March 1978, the newly branded U2 entered a talent contest hosted by Harp Lager and an Irish newspaper called the *Evening Press*, in the Irish city of Limerick. The band, which had struggled for two years to find its way, won the contest, earning them £500 (roughly $689) in prize money and studio time to record their first demo. The band's win also got them on the radar of CBS Records' Jackie Hayden, who judged the contest.

Winning the contest helped U2 convince a Dublin businessman, Paul McGuinness, to manage them. Since its inception, the band had been operating without official management or representation; Adam Clayton had been serving as the band's unofficial manager.[3]

U2 performed at the Limerick contest without Dick, who was older than the others and attending college. The band was consistently leaning toward a core group of four. Dick and his younger brother, Edge, both played guitar. Dick's presence became redundant. Dick played his last concert with the band in 1978 and Edge became U2's lead guitarist.

Three years after forming, U2—pictured here at a 1979 gig at the University of Leeds in England—was still playing small shows across Ireland and Britain.

Settled on the name U2 and on a core group of four members, with proper management, U2 began to book and play as many shows in and around Dublin as possible. All the band's members were finally out of school by 1978, allowing them to focus on developing their musical skills and lyrical abilities. With some studio time under their belts, the band released its first single, "U2:3" in September 1979. The single was an Irish-only release and topped Ireland's national charts.[4] Knowing they needed to strike out of Ireland to have a chance at real fame, U2 followed its successful Irish release of "U2:3" with a performance in London in December 1979. There, the band failed to gain significant attention from fans and critics alike.

Following the unsuccessful London performance, the band returned home to Dublin and limited its focus to building an Irish fan base. They released a successful second Irish-only single called "Another Day" in February 1980, on the same day they played at National Stadium in Dublin. Fortuitously, an agent for Island Records, Bill Stewart, was in attendance. Impressed by U2's performance, Stewart reported back to Island Records, which signed the band to its first international contract the following month. Within a few months, U2 released its first international single, "11 O'Clock Tick Tock," which failed to even make it on the musical charts. Seeking a solution to the band's flailing success, Island Records assigned a new producer, Steve Lillywhite, to work with U2. Lillywhite had a reputation as a somewhat unorthodox musical artist, and he was pivotal in the band's development. He produced U2's first three albums.

Boy: Four Young Men Show Their Conviction with First Album

Four years after U2 formed, with a recording contract and a new producer on board, the band finally released its debut

The year 1980 was an interesting time for music. The disco era of the 1970s had died out, but the decade had given rise to new kinds of rock, such as glam, hard/arena, heavy metal, and punk. Some mainstream musicians began incorporating reggae into their sound. Music in the 1970s became more electronic with heavy use of synthesizers and harmonizers. When the 1980s began, so did a new kind of popular music that relied heavily on synthesizers, "synthpop." This pop phenomenon instantly took hold of the decade's pop scene while rock music was dominated by hard-rocking arena bands. While the era's biggest acts enjoyed commercial success singing about typical themes such as love and loss and using new musical techniques, few were singing about conflict, such as the Cold War, which was entering its fourth decade, and the continued Irish-British conflict.

U2 was about to change everything.

The synthesizer, an electronic musical instrument, was popular in 1980s music.

full album, *Boy*, in October 1980. The album's song lyrics center on themes of personal and spiritual growth, faith, and mortality; for instance, one of its breakout hits, "I Will Follow," is about the death of Bono's mother.

The album is notable for addressing heavy subject matter that even veteran musicians didn't address in their music. It was also notable for its sound, which was not entirely hard

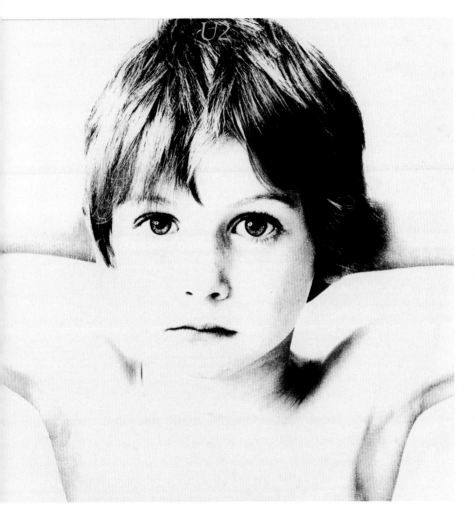

Boy, U2's debut album, achieved moderate success and brought the band on its first tour outside of Ireland and Britain.

The Early Years

On their debut album, U2 touched on themes such as innocence, growing up, sexuality, and becoming adults. The band's members were still very young, falling at about nineteen and twenty years of age during the album's recording and release. Though not the political powerhouse U2's later albums would be, *Boy* was still thematically advanced compared to most of the music of the era's other bands. The album even featured literary references to *Lord of the Flies* and *The Picture of Dorian Grey*.

Musically, Lillywhite helped U2 explore their instruments and their recording space. He employed unorthodox methods such as recording Mullen's drumming in the studio's stairwell to achieve a "clattery sound." Edge recorded all the songs using his Gibson Explorer guitar. To highlight certain themes, Lillywhite applied different feels to every song—for instance, an atmospheric sound for "Twilight," which is about entering adolescence.

rock, nor entirely pop. U2's first album immediately set them apart from their 1980 counterparts.

Boy sold nearly two hundred thousand copies in its initial release and peaked at sixty-three on the Billboard 200 list.[5]

Though largely unknown outside of Ireland and the United Kingdom, *Boy* struck a chord with the American gay community, in which the album enjoyed popularity. Bono has

A young boy's face is on the *Boy* album cover to represent its themes of adolescence and innocence.

attributed this to the album having a "sexual" nature and the homosexual audience responding well to its lyrics, though the band did not intentionally write any lyrics aimed at the homosexual community. Its popularity among the community led to some misconceptions about *Boy* being written for or by homosexuals. As socially conscious individuals, U2's members weren't fazed by these misconceptions, and the band embarked on its first official tour outside of Ireland and the United Kingdom.[6]

The *Boy* tour helped U2 develop fan bases in Europe and the United States, where they played well-attended and well-received club shows.

After U2's later success, *Boy* reentered the American music charts, setting off another round of interest in the album and the band behind it.

U2 had arrived with *Boy*, even if on a relatively small scale. The boys who had formed the band four years earlier were now young men who'd endured many frustrations, some highs, and some near-devastating lows. Their struggle to come to grips with the world was going to soon become apparent to everyone.

Fate, Faith, "Fire," and Flags

Following the *Boy* tour, U2 followed a rocky path in the pursuit of success. Though *Boy* had been well received and they'd played reasonably well-attended shows on the *Boy* tour, the band had a long way to go before "U2" became a household name.

"Fire" in October

The fateful twists began on the *Boy* tour, which the band had undertaken as young men with very little support or guidance from their record label. At a March 1981 nightclub performance in Portland, Oregon, Bono lost a briefcase of lyric and music ideas for U2's next album. This left U2 scrambling for material for their next album, and they had limited time to develop more before they had to begin recording their second album in July 1981. Still not entirely professional as far as musicians go and having lost the bulk of their ideas in Oregon, U2 had to improvise much of their work for their second album, *October*.

October's lead single track, "Fire," was released during the summer of 1981. "Fire" succeeded in making it onto the United

Kingdom's most popular songs chart and was the band's first-ever song to chart. This success garnered U2 an invitation to perform on the popular show *Top of the Pops*. However, "Fire" quickly fell on the charts.[1] The single's flash-in-the-pan success wasn't the only disappointment the summer of 1981 had for U2.

After losing much of their musical and lyrical ideas for their second album, *October,* U2's band members, here in 1981, had to scramble to get the album recorded and released on time.

Fate, Faith, "Fire," and Flags

In 1981, U2 opened for Irish rock band Thin Lizzy, pictured here, at Slane Castle in Ireland. U2's members have called the performance one of their worst.

The summer of 1981 was a poignant one in Ireland. Irish republican prisoners being held in Northern Ireland were on a second hunger strike (the first, in 1980, lasted fifty-three days). The hunger strike was a protest aimed at British prime minister Margaret Thatcher over the withdrawal of traditional prisoner of war privileges and treatment. Some of the protestors starved themselves for more than seventy days; ten of them died. The strike galvanized support for the Irish republican cause and radicalized its politics in an already violent conflict.[2] When the Anglo-Irish lord of Slane Castle, Henry Mount Charles, in County Meath, Ireland, announced an open-air concert in the natural amphitheater between the castle and the nearby River Boyne, both the lord and locals were fearful of what the Troubles might bring on the event. The concert was the first of many that would be held at Slane Castle and featured bands from Northern Ireland and the

Fate, Faith, "Fire," and Flags

Republic of Ireland, as well as some bands from around the globe. More than seventeen thousand fans showed up for the concert, where U2 opened for Irish hard rock band Thin Lizzy.[3]

U2 gave a mediocre performance at Slane. Edge has called the show one of the worst the band ever played, and years later, in 2001, when U2 returned to Slane to perform, Bono

A Crisis of Faith

Rock and roll has a reputation for hard-living musicians who get sucked into the trappings of fame. As U2 suffered through 1981, Bono, Edge, and Mullen began to question whether they could be in rock and roll and be Christian at the same time. Their doubts stemmed from their involvement in a charismatic Christian group called Shalom Fellowship. Bono and Edge practically quit U2 as they struggled with their faith and their chosen career. Eventually, they quit the Fellowship instead, resolving they could reconcile their religious and spiritual beliefs with being in U2. Though they teetered on breaking up during this crisis of faith, the decision to continue their musical careers while maintaining their beliefs was monumental: it defined much of their future music, which became inclusive of ideas about spirituality and faith. What nearly shattered U2 instead strengthened them and set them apart from their peers as they faced the 1980s.

admitted to the audience that the band's first performance at the castle had been bad.

Shaken by the loss of their lyrics and music at the Portland show in March 1981, the improvisation of much of the album *October*—which was released in October of that year and still holds the band's record for least popular album—and their bad show at Slane Castle, U2 was in a commercial crisis. It wasn't the only crisis U2 dealt with that year.

The sophomore slump of *October*, a turbulent Ireland, and the crises of career and faith had the potential to end U2. Losing the music and lyrics in Portland had caused chaos for the young band members. Bono couldn't believe someone would be so callous as to steal his hard work from backstage, making him question what he was doing in U2. (The briefcase of lost music and lyrics was returned to Bono by fan Danielle Rheaume in 2004. Her friend, Cindy Harris, found the briefcase in the attic of a house she rented in Tacoma, Washington—a house that had once been rented by a roadie on the *Boy* tour, who took the briefcase for safekeeping but never successfully returned it to the band or the tour's promoters. Contrary to Bono's original, desperate suspicions, the briefcase had not been stolen.[4])

Facing their odds, the band had to get scrappy.

"There was a firm resolve to come out of the box fighting with the next record."[5]
—Adam Clayton

The Band Goes to War

U2 entered 1982 on the heels of the unpopular release of *October* in October 1981. With close to nothing to lose and

Fate, Faith, "Fire," and Flags

everything to gain, they tapped into the sociopolitical strife of the early 1980s and came out swinging with their third album, *War*, which was released in February 1983. The album was an outright attack on the fluffy, keyboard- and synthesizer-heavy music of the era, known then as the New Romantic movement. U2 had formed in the spirit of the anarchistic punk rock movement of the 1970s but came to prominence in the post-punk era. Edge mused about the musical dilemma U2 solved with *War* in a *Rolling Stone* article: "Punk had died. We couldn't believe it had been swept to the side as if it had never happened, and *War* was designed as a knuckle buster in the face of the new pop."[6]

With *War*, U2 turned "pacifism itself into a crusade."[7] —*New York Times*

Not wanting to lose their way in the maze of the new 1980s sounds, U2 opted to develop its own style. *War* was the band's unapologetic reintroduction to the world of music.

Aggressive in sound and lyrics, U2 came forward with their sociopolitical views on their third album. For the first time, the band directly addressed the Troubles in the song "Sunday Bloody Sunday." The same child who had appeared on the cover of the band's first album, *Boy*, was on *War*'s cover; this time, his expression was fearful instead of innocent.

The *War* tour was U2's first profitable tour. It brought U2 to bigger venues, and Bono became more theatrical in his performances. Bono waving a massive white flag— traditionally, a symbol of surrender or truce, but for Bono, a political statement of a flag drained of all that divides nations—during "Sunday Bloody Sunday" became the tour's iconic image. The band's June 5, 1983, Red Rocks concert in Colorado was named one of "50 Moments that Changed the

Musically and lyrically heavy, *War* focused on the physical and emotional impacts of war. Several songs on the album dealt with specific conflicts. "Sunday Bloody Sunday" was a protest song about the civil strife in U2's home nation of Ireland. "Seconds" criticized the proliferation of nuclear weapons, particularly within the context of the Cold War, which was entering its fourth decade of conflict. The Communist Soviet Union still crouched behind the Iron Curtain, posing an unknown threat to the Western world, while the United States ramped up its military might in response to the possibility of nuclear war. "New Years Day" was about the Polish Solidarity Movement, an antigovernment protest that was harshly punished by Poland's then-Communist government. U2 exploded on the world stage with an album no one saw coming: a militant sound coupled with desperate pleas for peace, cementing their reputation as one of the most politically vocal and active bands in history.

A French nuclear test takes place in 1970 in French Polynesia. The song "Seconds" on the *War* album was a criticism of the growth in nuclear weapons and the potential for nuclear warfare.

War's critical and commercial success raised U2's global profile and grew their audiences, as evidenced here at the 1983 US Festival in San Bernardino, California.

History of Rock and Roll" by *Rolling Stone* in 2004.[8] *War* got more extensive radio time due to its popularity, and the band was supported by a new medium, MTV, which had debuted in 1981. The album even managed to knock Michael Jackson's massively successful *Thriller* album from the top of UK charts.

U2's *War* was right on time: it rocketed the band into mainstream popularity at the same time their deal with Island Records was up for renegotiation in 1984. Due to the album's breakthrough popularity, U2 was able to sign a lucrative extension.

U2 had won the battle for recognition with *War*, but were they ready to wage war on fame?

Jumping into the Fire

In the four years since their first album, 1980's *Boy*, U2 did a lot of growing up. They'd seen professional ups and downs. They'd lost and regained their footing, musically and lyrically. They'd faced a crisis of faith that nearly broke up the band, only to storm the charts with the revelation that was *War*. Despite having seen much of the world, the band's members opted to keep Ireland their home base. In one of his first of many forays into the world of politics, Bono accepted then-Irish prime minister Garret FitzGerald's request to serve on a government committee on unemployment in 1984.

In their personal lives, much had transpired. In 1982, Bono married his high school sweetheart, Ali, to whom he's still married. Edge married his high school sweetheart, Aislinn, in 1983, and they had

"Unlike anyone else in rock & roll, U2 . . . addresses the most ignored—and most volatile—area of inquiry: alienation from religion."[1]
—*Rolling Stone*

their first child, Hollie, in 1984. Mullen continued his partnership with his longtime girlfriend, Ann Acheson, whom, like Bono's wife Ali and Edge's wife Aislinn, he'd met at Mount Temple Comprehensive School. (Mullen and Acheson have never married, but they're still together.) As U2 went into the studio to record their fourth album, *The Unforgettable Fire*, they were hot on the heels of *War*'s success and juggling personal and professional demands.

Bono and his wife, Ali, pictured here at Cork Airport in Ireland prior to a performance on the *Joshua Tree* tour in 1987, were high school sweethearts. They're still married today.

Jumping into the Fire

An Experimental Album

While the ink dried on their new and better deal with Island Records, U2—ever fearful of being cornered into a musical category—worried the rock-and-roll sound of *War* would stick with them and turn them into one of the 1980s' arena rock bands. Wanting to set themselves apart and stay committed to their sociopolitical messages, the band began experimenting with new sounds and lyrics in recording *The Unforgettable Fire*, which they partially recorded at Slane Castle, where they'd had a regrettable live performance just three years earlier. Edge and Clayton used inspiration from eccentric artists in creating the fourth album, making Island Records worry the band was going too avant-garde for continued success. The band came together on an abstract feel for the album, leaving much of it, even the lyrics, open to interpretation—for good or for bad—when it released in October 1984. While *The Unforgettable Fire* seems loose and meandering, some of the music and lyrics have U2's trademark passion and political lean, such as the lead single "Pride (In the Name of Love)," which Bono wrote about one of his heroes, American civil rights activist Martin Luther King Jr.

The tour for *The Unforgettable Fire* moved U2 into bigger indoor arenas and built their audience. They overcame the challenge of playing the album's more complex sounds onstage, and some of the album's critics even praised how the songs sounded better onstage than on the record.

U2's growing popularity and recognition couldn't have come at a better time for a band that wanted to grow its brand on something that mattered.

Playing Live Aid

U2, the band that imbued its principles and values into every record they ever made, had to make an impression in the one-time-only event that was Live Aid.

The Irish-based band, playing from a British venue in front of the world, kicked off its twenty-minute, three-song

Out of the Fire, into the Frying Pan

After bursting onto the scene with *War*, U2 got the attention of music critics—just in time for them to release another unpopular album. Some critics lauded *The Unforgettable Fire*'s experimental sound, but others weren't shy in their dislike for the band's fourth album. In a *Rolling Stone* review of the album, Kurt Loder expressed his disappointment: "U2 flickers and nearly fades, its fire banked by a misconceived production strategy and occasional interludes of soggy, songless self-indulgence. This is not a 'bad' album, but neither is it the irrefutable beauty the band's fans anticipated."[2] For the first but certainly not the last time, U2 was criticized for its moralizing and idealism.[3]

The band seemed destined for another *October* slump. This time, however, the entire world was watching.

Pictured here in Sydney, Australia, on their 1984 *Unforgettable Fire* tour, U2 was promoting their fourth album—which received very mixed reviews and was largely unpopular.

set with "Sunday Bloody Sunday," a song about historic incidents of violence between the British and the Irish, who fought for decades to gain independence from Britain. In the 1980s, spurts of violence frequently made headlines.

U2 then moved on to "Bad," a song written about losing loved ones to heroin addiction, an epidemic for which the 1980s famously suffered, but not a vice of U2 itself, as Edge explained in a 1985 *Rolling Stone* interview: "Drugs, and the whole idea of smoking dope and getting absolutely drunk, seemed to me like an unjustifiable activity. The whole drug culture is a criminal thing; the same guys who deal the marijuana are the guys who deal heroin, who break people's legs, who get thirteen-year-olds hooked. I felt no attraction to that side of it."[4]

The band played "Bad" for twelve minutes, during which Bono, seeing an audience member getting crushed by throngs of people, jumped into the crowd to embrace her. Later, the girl credited Bono with saving her life. The embrace was seen by the world, and the band's performance of "Bad" has been hailed as a breakthrough moment for U2—a good thing, considering

U2 stormed the world stage with their performance at 1985's globally televised charity concert Live Aid. Pictured here with bassist Adam Clayton at Live Aid, Bono stole the show with his performance style.

they didn't even get to perform the third song of their set, "Pride (In the Name of Love)." Bono pulled audience members onto the stage as U2 closed its set, and, for all intents and purposes, the front man behaved erratically throughout the band's first-ever international show. Thinking they'd flunked their high-stakes Live Aid concert, U2 left England feeling

"For a growing number of rock-and-roll fans, U2 have become the band that matters most, maybe even the only band that matters."[5] —*Rolling Stone*

U2

On July 13, 1985, two epic concerts—one at Philadelphia's JFK Stadium and one at London's Wembley Stadium—were performed by dozens of the world's biggest musical stars. The reason? To raise money for African famine relief. At Wembley, legends such as David Bowie, Pete Townshend of the Who, and the Beatles' Paul McCartney took the stage, as did some of the decade's most popular bands, such as Queen and Wham!. In London, these musical greats performed in front of a huge live audience that included Prince Charles and Princess Diana. Both the London and Philadelphia concerts were watched by more than one billion television viewers around the world. U2 was invited to perform at Live Aid during *The Unforgettable Fire* tour, and there, they met some of the world's biggest music icons at a concert performed solely for a greater cause.

gloomy. Within days, however, they learned many spectators thought their Live Aid performance was the day's highlight.

Later that year, U2 was named "Band of the '80s" by *Rolling Stone*.[6]

Rejuvenated by Live Aid, U2 joined the Conspiracy of Hope Tour benefiting Amnesty International in 1986.[7] Now a household name, U2 entered a public tug-of-war between commercial success and lofty ideals.

Crossing the Desert Ends in Rattled Nerves

Despite the lukewarm reception to their fourth album, *The Unforgettable Fire*, in 1984, U2 was reinvigorated by the world's reception to their iconic performance at the historic Live Aid concert in July 1985. Live Aid's charitable mission was right up U2's alley, they'd been named "Band of the '80s" by *Rolling Stone*, and they spent part of 1986 on the Conspiracy of Hope Tour benefiting Amnesty International. The positive attention from fans and critics and the opportunity to participate in major philanthropic endeavors gave U2 a renewed energy when they began recording their fifth studio album, *Joshua Tree*, in 1986.

Joshua *Tree* was released in March 1987 despite Bono's last-minute panic about the album's quality. He had little to worry about, however: the album received platinum certification in the United Kingdom within forty-eight hours of its release—the fastest-selling album in British chart history.

It debuted at number one on the UK Albums chart, staying at the top for two weeks, and it stayed on the chart for a total of 201 weeks. On the US *Billboard* Top Pop Albums chart, the album debuted at number seven and reached number one within three weeks. *Joshua Tree* spent 120 weeks on the *Billboard* chart, 35 of those in the top ten, and in May 1987, the Recording Industry Association of America certified the album double platinum. This success allowed all of U2's previous albums to reenter the *Billboard* chart. Its success landed U2 on the cover of *Time* magazine; they were the fourth rock band to ever get a *Time* cover story. In 1988, the album won the Grammy for Album of the Year and Best Rock Performance by a Duo or Group with Vocal.[1] Critics and fans loved the album, and to this day, it remains the band's gold standard.

One thing was abundantly clear: the world wanted more of the band that had made history at Live Aid.

Many critics hailed the album as the first in which U2 finally found its focus and pinned down its unique sound. On the album, Edge's guitar was characteristic of what would go on to be his trademark sound, using delay effects alongside his traditional simplistic style. Bono, too, experimented with his singing style, much to the delight of critics, who found his matured vocals dynamic, passionate, and expressive of the complex themes *Joshua Tree* explores.

The Angst Behind the Success

A simple listen to *Joshua Tree* reveals U2's gritty but sensitive approach to its longstanding commitment to music with a purpose. The album alternates between soaring, gospel-like anthems such as "Where the Streets Have No Name" and "I Still Haven't Found What I'm Looking For," both characterized by upbeat music overlaid by Bono's impassioned lyrics about the search for meaning and answers in life, and heavily personal and haunting songs such as "With or Without You," in which Bono agonizes over the vulnerability of relationships. The critical darling and commercial success that was *Joshua Tree* came at a high price, however.

As ever, sociopolitical frustrations were the basis for much of the album. By the time they settled into the studio to record *Joshua Tree*, U2 had toured extensively around the world. Bono was devastated by the despair and violence he saw in many nations. On a visit to El Salvador in the early 1980s, he witnessed the bloody Salvadoran Civil War, which lasted twelve years and claimed more than seventy thousand lives. The conflict arose between a militant oligarchy (supported financially by the administration of US president Ronald Reagan) that dominated resources and a group of communist revolutionaries made up of mostly impoverished peasants and poor urban workers seeking opportunity and social justice.[2] Like many Irish, Bono had long harbored a romanticized view of America; in the nineteenth and early twentieth century, millions of Irish immigrated to America to escape the poverty, starvation, and oppressive British rule in Ireland. Learning that America supported a brutal regime in El Salvador shattered some of Bono's adoration of the United States, which he expressed in two *Joshua Tree* songs: "Bullet the Blue Sky" and "Mothers of the Disappeared."

The UK miners' strike of the mid-1980s (a strike that attempted to prevent the conservative government, led by Prime Minister Margaret Thatcher, from closing coal mines), inspired the striker-sympathetic song "Red Hill Mining Town." The heroin epidemic of the 1980s was addressed in "Running to Stand Still," and "Where the Streets Have No Name" was

U2 shot the Grammy Award–winning video for "Where the Streets Have No Name" atop a building in downtown Los Angeles.

The Joshua tree is a yucca plant found primarily in the Mojave Desert, which stretches across part of the American Southwest. According to legend, Mormon settlers in the West named these trees after a biblical figure, Joshua, who reaches his hands toward the sky in prayer.[3] U2 learned about the trees in December 1986 while on a photo shoot in the American Southwest. The band was ending a difficult year, which they likened to a "desert," and their upcoming album was heavy with references to the year's challenges. When Bono learned the religious significance of the Joshua tree, he determined it was the perfect name and symbol for their upcoming album. *"Joshua Tree* takes its title from the tree that somehow survives in the desert, and much of its material suggests an attempt, within the aridity, to quench a profoundly spiritual thirst."[4]

A yucca plant found mostly in the American Southwest desert, U2 saw the Joshua tree as the perfect symbol for their hugely popular and successful 1987 album.

inspired by the continued violence in Northern Ireland—specifically, around the idea that in the capital of Belfast, a person's religion and background, which were divisive and deadly factors in the Troubles, could be determined simply by the street on which they lived.

Joshua Tree wasn't just about the state of global politics. On a personal level, 1986 was a challenging year for U2. Bono's marriage to his high school sweetheart, Ali, was strained, likely due to the demands of touring and recording; "With

Alienation at Home

U2's participation in the May 1986 Self Aid concert, a benefit concert that raised millions for a job-creation trust fund and more than one thousand jobs in Ireland (all profits from the concert and its subsequent album went to the Self Aid Trust), was met with criticism by the Irish media. The Self Aid backlash showed U2 that though they'd conquered the world, their home nation harbored resentment for them: some Republic of Ireland diehards hated U2 because the band openly opposed Noraid, an organization that funded the Irish Republic Army during the Troubles[5]; others weren't pleased by what they perceived as a searing indictment of Ireland's religious and political divisions in songs such as "Sunday Bloody Sunday." U2 began to feel unwelcome in their own country.

or Without You" is widely perceived to be about his marital discord. U2's beloved assistant, Greg Carroll, was killed in a motorcycle accident in July 1986 (*Joshua Tree* is dedicated to Carroll, and the song "One Tree Hill," is about the band's grief over losing him).

U2 Rattles Downward

On the heels of *Joshua Tree*'s immense success, U2 embarked on a two-pronged concept for their sixth studio album, *Rattle and Hum*, which was released in October 1988 and inspired by their experiences in America on the *Joshua Tree* tour. The concept involved a double studio album that was heavily influenced by American blues, folk rock, and gospel music, and a companion "rockumentary" (a documentary about a rock group) documenting their time in America on the *Joshua Tree* tour. The album was a collection of new songs, live performances, and covers of songs by rock greats such as the Beatles and Bob Dylan. Partially recorded in Memphis, Tennessee, the album includes collaborations with Bob Dylan, blues legend B. B. King, and a gospel choir from Harlem. The rockumentary, initially paid for by the band—who wanted it to be a low-budget film shown in a small number of theaters— was bought by Hollywood powerhouse Paramount Pictures, which turned the film into a large-scale production.

The critics were scathing.

Though U2 intended to pay tribute to rock legends on *Rattle and Hum*, critics accused the band of deliberately trying to edge its way into rock legend status. A *Rolling Stone* reviewer called the album "misguided and bombastic."[6] A *New York Times* reviewer went even further: "The album bounces from stadium anthems to new studio recordings and snippets. The plan, clearly, was to retain the moral fervor of 'The Joshua Tree,' yet to vary U2's much imitated style, to pay homage to American music, and to regain some of the spontaneity that

Crossing the Desert Ends in Rattled Nerves

U2 brings the audience behind the scenes in the 1988 *Rattle and Hum* rockumentary that accompanied the band's sixth album of the same name.

superstar status can crush. Unfortunately, the band's self-importance got in the way. 'Rattle and Hum' is plagued by U2's attempts to grab every mantle in the Rock-and-Roll Hall of Fame . . . Each attempt is embarrassing in a different way."[7]

Movie review duo Roger Ebert and Gene Siskel were split on the *Rattle and Hum* film; Ebert called it monotonous, while Siskel liked the music and was moved by footage of the Harlem gospel choir with which U2 collaborated. U2 was aware the film project didn't follow their artistic vision once Hollywood got involved, as Edge explained: "*Rattle and Hum* was conceived as a scrapbook, a memento of that time spent in America on the Joshua Tree tour. It changed when the movie, which was initially conceived of as a low-budget film, suddenly became a big Hollywood affair. That put a different emphasis on the album, which suffered from the huge promotion and publicity, and people reacted against it."[8] Amid the negative reviews were a few positive reviews that lauded the album's music and the spirit of the rockumentary, and despite the criticism it received, the album was a success. It stayed at the number one spot on America's *Billboard* 200 chart for six weeks and made it to the number one spot on UK and Australian charts. *Rolling Stone*, which published a scathing review of the album after it was released, included *Rattle and Hum* on its 2014 list of the 40 Greatest Rock Documentaries.[9] Other harsh critics have, in the years that have passed, revisited their original reviews of the album and shown more generosity and understanding for *Rattle and Hum*.

The band embarked on the Lovetown Tour (1989–1990) to promote *Rattle and Hum*, but only toured Australasia, Japan, and Europe; they stayed away from America altogether to avoid further backlash from critics. The *Rattle and Hum* misery had company: internally, the band was in discord as its members became unhappy with their live performances and disagreed on musical direction. In August 1989, Clayton made headlines after being arrested in Dublin for possession of marijuana, and Edge's marriage was on the rocks.

Stung by the criticism for *Rattle and Hum* and facing the end of a momentous decade that had been alternatingly harsh and kind to them, U2's future was uncertain. At the end of a December 30, 1989, concert, Bono hinted that the band was at the end of their journey. "This is just the end of something for U2. And that's what we're playing these concerts—and we're throwing a party for ourselves and you. It's no big deal, it's just—we have to go away and ... and dream it all up again."[10]

Crossing the Desert Ends in Rattled Nerves

Returning to Their Roots: Geopolitical Reunification Revives U2

With the disappointment of *Rattle and Hum* hanging over their heads and internal discord plaguing the band that had doggedly persevered for fourteen years, U2 entered the 1990s facing, basically, two options: break up the band or find a new angle to keep moving forward. They faced challenges outside the band, too; for instance, after seven years of marriage that produced three children, Edge and his wife, Aislinn, separated in 1990 and entered a lengthy divorce process.

Ever the political band, U2 turned to a major world event to save them: the fall of the Berlin Wall in November 1989. The wall had separated East and West Germany since 1961, when it was built by the Communist government of the German Democratic Republic to keep Westerners and their influence from entering East Germany and undermining the socialist state, as well as to prevent mass defections from East to West. As the Soviet Union began to dissolve at the end of the 1980s, the East German Communist Party announced in November 1989 that East German citizens could, for the first time in nearly thirty years, cross the border. Berlin was the center of celebrations as East and West Germans reunited and began hacking down the wall that had, for all those decades, stood as an unmoving symbol of the divisive Cold War.[1]

U2 saw German reunification as a metaphor for their own reunification. They flew to Berlin in 1990 to participate

After nearly thirty years of dividing Europe, the Berlin Wall fell in 1989. U2 arrived on the scene shortly after, seeking inspiration for their next album.

Returning to Their Roots: Geopolitical Reunification Revives U2

in the revelry surrounding the fall of the Berlin Wall, to find inspiration in German reunification, and to begin recording their seventh studio album, *Achtung Baby*, at Berlin's Hansa Studios.

Achtung is German for "caution" or "watch out."

The Berlin Sessions

While a strong metaphor for the band's own needs, being onsite for the fall of the Berlin Wall went south quickly. The band ended up in a terrible motel after the East German house they'd rented was retaken by its owners, who'd been in Western Europe when the wall went up and now returned home after thirty years.[2] They found the mood in Berlin less celebratory than they'd anticipated and hoped for; West Berliners were fearful for their livelihoods as their East Berlin counterparts, impoverished by long years in the deteriorating Soviet Union, were brought back into the fold. East Berliners were unconvinced the fall of the wall actually heralded the dissolution of the Soviet Union. Others, still committed to the Soviets and Communism, didn't welcome the reunification.

The studio, which U2 chose because David Bowie had recorded some seminal work there in the 1970s, had fallen into disrepair as the Soviet Union deteriorated around it. The recording sessions were full of division; members didn't agree on musical direction and quality. Clayton and Mullen preferred U2's usual sound, while Bono and Edge wanted to introduce

"One" is the namesake for Bono's charitable organization, the ONE Campaign.

U2

After internal strife caused U2's members to retreat into their respective corners at Hansa, some improvised chords strummed by Edge caught the others' attention and birthed the breakthrough they needed. The song, "One," would go on to be one of the most popular songs in history, and the personal nature of its lyrics and vulnerability of its sound symbolized *Achtung Baby*'s thematic departure from U2's usual sociopolitical themes and militant sound. The band has called this departure "four men chopping down the Joshua Tree,"[3] meaning a departure from the ideologically driven music for which the band is generally known.

Haunting in everything from its somber opening chords to Bono's lyrical escalation from defeat to evident desperation, "One" was written to describe German reunification. The personal nature of its lyrics, however, has been interpreted by many as a description of the band's close call with breaking up.

European industrial music and electronic dance music. The band nearly broke up in Berlin, until an improvised song saved them—a song that would fly to the top of the charts and catapult the band into a hugely successful decade.

Following the "One" breakthrough, U2 returned to Dublin in 1991 to finish *Achtung*. There, their relationships improved, and the album was completed with a new sound for U2, one that incorporated alternative rock, industrial music, and even electronic dance music. Edge explained the band's desire to explore a new sound: "We're at a point where production has gotten so slick that people don't trust it anymore . . . We were starting to lose trust in the conventional sound of rock & roll— the conventional sound of guitar . . . those big reverb-laden drum sounds of the '80s or those big, beautiful, pristine vocal sounds with all this lush ambience and reverb. So we found ourselves searching for other sounds that had more life and more freshness."[4]

Achtung Baby was released in November 1991 and is, to this day, one of U2's most successful records. The album was well received and got favorable reviews, debuting at number one on the US *Billboard* 200 Top Albums chart and topping the charts

Pictured here on their *Zoo TV* tour, U2—especially Bono—used theatrics and elaborate, ironic props to comment on pop culture and media.

Returning to Their Roots: Geopolitical Reunification Revives U2

Zoo TV was staged as an elaborate commentary on media oversaturation's role in desensitizing people. Inspired by the then-fledgling twenty-four-hour news cycle, Gulf War coverage, and media-overloaded and often inane morning radio shows (called "morning zoo"), U2 served its audience sensory overload. The stage had dozens of large video screens that constantly flicked between disparate visuals, video clips, and flashing text. Bono conceived and portrayed a number of characters to make a statement about the media icons of the day: "The Fly" was a leather-clad egomaniac; "Mirror Ball Man" was a greedy televangelist; and "MacPhisto" was a devilish character for which Bono sported red horns. Though U2 sought to be more lighthearted with Zoo TV than they'd been on other tours, the principled band still found a way to make sociopolitical statements through irony, humor, and mocking mass media.

Bono's Mister MacPhisto persona, pictured here at London's Wembley Arena on the Zoo TV tour, was one of multiple personas U2's frontman adopted to make political and social statements.

in many other countries. Five songs were released as commercial singles and all were chart successes. The album won a Grammy Award in 1993 for Best Rock Performance by a Duo or Group with Vocal, and critics have hailed it one of the greatest albums of all time.

Zoo TV

Seeking to continue disrupting their methods and to surprise fans, U2 launched the elaborate Zoo TV tour (1992–1993) to promote *Achtung*. Instead of U2's usual spartan sets, Zoo TV was elaborate in everything from stage scenery to stage presence. Bono introduced ironic, highly dramatized personas and pulled pranks from stage, such as calling then-president George Bush and the United Nations. The band provided live satellite links of the tour to Sarajevo, the capital of Bosnia and Herzegovina, which was torn apart by civil war.

The tour was wildly successful, although the band had to face Clayton's problems with alcohol when, one night, he was too hungover to perform.[5] A stand-in bassist took the stage with U2 that night, marking the only time the four core members weren't onstage together for a show. While Edge was embroiled in a lengthy divorce from his wife, Aislinn, in 1993 he began dating Morleigh Steinberg, who belly danced onstage during the tour's performances of "Mysterious Ways." (Edge and Steinberg would eventually marry in 2002 after having two children together.)

Zoo TV was the highest-grossing North American tour of 1992 and sold more than five million tickets over its five legs. The band's eighth studio album, *Zooropa*, recorded in 1993 during a break in the Zoo TV tour, expanded on the tour's mass media themes. *Zooropa*'s songs were played in Zoo TV's 1993 performances. A 1994 film about the tour, *Zoo TV: Live from Sydney*, won a Grammy.

Returning to Their Roots: Geopolitical Reunification Revives U2

With *Achtung Baby*, Zoo TV, and *Zooropa*, U2 struck a long-needed balance: principled but accessible. In 1993, U2 signed a six-album deal to stay with Island Records/PolyGram, and *Zooropa* won the Grammy for Best Alternative Music Album in 1994. Despite the failings of *Rattle and Hum* and the band's Berlin stay, U2 was back on top of the world by the mid-90s.

U2

Speeding Toward the Millennium and Beyond

Following the success of *Achtung Baby* and *Zoo TV*, U2 took a break from recording and touring. They returned in 1995 with a chart-topping single on that year's *Batman Forever* soundtrack and an experimental album, *Original Soundtracks 1*, released under the name Passengers so the public would distinguish it from the band's usual albums. Unsurprisingly, it wasn't a commercial success, but U2 was at the point where they could indulge themselves in new methods and pop right back up—which they did with *Pop*, their ninth studio album.

The Highs and Lows of Pop

Pop began recording in 1995 but didn't release until 1997; the band spent much of 1996 reworking their material. *Pop* indulged the band in a previous endeavor to introduce nightclub-style sounds into their music. The album was either met very favorably or very

U2's PopMart tour continued the elaborate themes and social statements introduced in Zoo TV while introducing the band's incorporation of nightclub-style music. This was met with mixed reviews.

Sarajevo

In September 1997, U2 played in Sarajevo, in the southern European country of Bosnia and Herzegovina, on their PopMart Tour. They were the first major musical artist to play there following the end of the Bosnian War, an armed conflict in which tens of thousands of people were killed and more than two million were displaced in the war's horrific ethnic cleansing campaigns.[1] U2 offered to hold a benefit concert or a small show but happily gave in to fans' requests to instead stage a full-on PopMart concert. The show peacefully brought together people who came from ethnic groups that clashed during the war. The Associated Press wrote afterward, "For two magical hours, the rock band U2 achieved what warriors, politicians and diplomats could not: They united Bosnia."[2]

poorly by critics, and while it debuted at number one in more than thirty countries, it quickly fell from the charts. The PopMart tour found U2 back in their element of making social statements; the tour was a satire of consumerism. The tour wasn't a great success story, except for one instance in which the band leaned into their old sociopolitical ways.

The year 2000 marked twenty years since the release of U2's first album, *Boy*. In anticipation of this milestone, U2 released its first official compilation in 1998. *The Best of 1980–1990* enjoyed the highest first-week sales of any greatest-hits record in the United States.

U2 has called the Sarajevo concert one of the proudest moments of their career.

Taking on the Millennium

As the year 2000 approached, U2 looked back on all the transitional sounds in their 1990s music and decided to simplify their sound. To do so, they took a hard look at themselves as a band and returned to a simple method: a band playing together in a room, not a band introducing complex methods, themes, and sounds. Following this methodology, the band began recording their tenth album, *All That You Can't Leave Behind*, in 1998. During this time, the band began to feel the constraints of working around Bono's political and philanthropic schedule, a factor that would become constant. While recording *All That You Can't Leave Behind*, Bono split his time between U2 and his efforts for the Jubilee 2000 debt relief project.

Compounded by Bono's philanthropic schedule and the band members' individual commitments to spend more time with their families, recording for *All That You Can't Leave Behind* lasted two years; the album wasn't released until October 2000.

With *All That You Can't Leave Behind*, U2 ushered in the millennium with success. *Rolling Stone* called it their third masterpiece (the first two being *The Joshua Tree* and *Achtung Baby*). It debuted at number one in thirty-two countries, and its lead single, "Beautiful Day," was a huge hit, winning the Grammy for Song of the Year, Best Rock Performance by a Duo or Group with Vocal, and Record of the Year. In 2001, U2 embarked on the Elevation Tour, during which they returned to smaller arena performances after years of larger stadium concerts. In doing so, the band returned to another U2 basic: connecting with their fans on a more personal level.

Bono delivers a speech at the fourth Tokyo International Conference on African Development in 2008. He has long been involved in political and charitable causes.

The Bono Conundrum

Lots of people don't like U2, chiefly because of front man Bono. Intense, earnest, passionate, and eager, Bono has been perceived by many as arrogant and sanctimonious throughout the band's long history. While Bono sees his celebrity as the opportunity to make positive change in the world, his critics accuse him of exploiting charitable causes to increase his celebrity.

Throughout his career, Bono has expanded his philanthropic efforts beyond lyrics to include— just to name a few—working with the United Nations, meeting with world leaders to discuss diplomatic issues, and cofounding ONE and (RED), organizations that fight AIDS and extreme poverty. Since the late 1990s, U2's schedule has had to adjust around Bono's always-increasing calendar of philanthropic efforts. However, U2 supports Bono's work, knowing first-hand how far he's come from scrappy Dublin street kid to global activist.

Love him or hate him, there's no denying that Bono has spent his fame working for others.

U2, 9/11, and Unprecedented Success

All That You Can't Leave Behind was a personal album, as far as U2 albums go. Many of its songs address family, friendship, love, death, and renewal. Several of the album's songs showed an almost eerie premonition on U2's part. Within a year of the album's release, New York City and the Pentagon outside Washington, DC, were attacked by terrorists on September 11, 2001, killing thousands of innocent people. The lyrics in several songs from *All That You Can't Leave Behind* took on new meaning for Americans struggling to cope with their post–September 11 grief, namely: "New York," which Bono has called a tribute to Frank Sinatra; "Stuck in a Moment You Can't Get Out Of," which was written about the 1997 suicide of Bono's friend Michael Hutchence, lead singer of the popular band INXS; "Peace on Earth," which was inspired by the devastating August 1998 Omagh bombing in Northern Ireland; and "Walk On," written about Aung San Suu Kyi, a Burmese woman who was placed under house arrest for twenty-one years (1989–2010) for her pro-democracy activities.[3]

Ironically, the always-political U2 wasn't trying to make sociopolitical statements with songs like "New York" and "Stuck in a Moment You Can't Get Out Of"; by simply being honest and vulnerable without trying to be overly earnest, U2 achieved sociopolitical statements anyway.

Just one month after the September 11 attacks, U2 played Madison Square Garden in New York City. In February 2002, U2 was the Super Bowl XXXVI halftime performer, an opportunity the band used to pay tribute to September 11 victims by displaying their names on a backdrop.

Everyone from music critics to the NFL called U2's halftime show the best in Super Bowl history.[4]

Speeding Toward the Millennium and Beyond

Pictured here at the 2002 Super Bowl in New Orleans, U2 was the game's coveted halftime performer. The band displayed September 11 victims' names during their performance.

Later in 2002, U2 earned more Grammy Awards for *All That You Can't Leave Behind*: Best Rock Album, and the song "Walk On" was awarded Record of the Year. This was the first time an artist won Record of the Year consecutively for songs from one album.[5]

Late in 2002, U2 released their second compilation, *The Best of 1990–2000*. The compilation included two new tracks, showing that U2 didn't intend to rest on their laurels, even after twenty-six years of continuous recording and touring.

CHAPTER 8

Reviving Old Themes, Embracing New Technology, and Making History

For their eleventh studio album, U2 wanted a harder rock sound than they'd produced in their last few albums, as well as a return to topics such as war and faith. In November 2004, *How to Dismantle an Atomic Bomb* was released and received favorably, reaching number one in thirty countries. U2 began recording the album in February 2003; after nine months, they had enough material for the album, but wanting to ensure a return to the hard rock sound and hard-hitting issues of their earlier work, the band spent another six months with producer Steve Lillywhite reworking the music and how they performed it. Bono called it the band's "first rock album. It's taken us twenty years or whatever it is, but this is our first rock album."[1] U2's traditional themes of faith, love, war, and family—the

In their very first year of eligibility, U2 was inducted into the Rock and Roll Hall of Fame in 2005.

last item being a growing area of interest for Bono, Edge, and Mullen as their own families grew—are prominent on *How to Dismantle an Atomic Bomb*, which sold more than ten million copies and made it onto *Rolling Stone*'s list of the "100 Best Albums of the Decade."

While embracing and adapting to music's changing landscape, U2 continued to make history. In March 2005, the band was inducted into the Rock and Roll Hall of Fame in their very first year of eligibility. All the band's members were in their mid-forties at the time of induction. Even after so many years of recording and touring, U2 showed no sign of retiring from the business. In fact, that same year, U2 embarked on the Vertigo Tour (2005–2006) to promote *How to Dismantle an Atomic Bomb*. The tour got off to a rough start; Edge's daughter suffered an illness and online presales were problematic, delaying the tour's start. However, the tour finally commenced and was successful; the band even brought back old songs they hadn't performed live in many years.

In August 2005, a devastating hurricane named Katrin slammed into the southeastern United States, inflictin large-scale damage in states such as Mississippi an Louisiana. A year later, U2 teamed up with alternativ rock band Green Day to record a cover of "The Saints Ar Coming" (a song with lyrics about storms and drownin originally released in 1979 by Scottish punk band Skids for Katrina-related charities. On September 25, 2006 both bands performed the cover live during the *Monda Night Football* pregame show of the New Orleans Saints first game in the Louisiana Superdome after the stadiun was ravaged in Hurricane Katrina. They also performe Green Day's "Wake Me Up When September Ends," U2' "Beautiful Day," and "The House of the Rising Sun," folk song about New Orleans. In November 2005, Edg created the charity Music Rising to buy new instrumen for New Orleans musicians affected by Katrina, helping the city uphold its rich musical traditions.[2]

Hurricane Katrina devastated large swathes of the American Southeast. New Orleans, pictured here in Katrina's wake, was one of the storm's notable victims.

Slow Start to Next Album

After wrapping up the Vertigo tour and Hurricane Katrina efforts, U2 began recording their eleventh album, *No Line on the Horizon*, with producer Rick Rubin in 2006. U2 spent just two weeks working on songs with Rubin at London's iconic Abbey Road Studios, best known as the Beatles' recording studio, before abandoning recording. In January of the following year, Bono made it clear that that U2—in true U2 fashion—wanted their new album to go in a new musical direction. The band shelved the music recorded with Rubin and returned to two producers they'd worked with for years, Brian Eno and Daniel Lanois, in May 2007 in Morocco, where they spent two weeks recording in a riad, a traditional Moroccan house with an interior garden or courtyard, and investigating local music. The band's members saw this as a return to their old ways of exploring new sounds in new places. They continued to record the album in New York, London, and Dublin.[3]

No Line on the Horizon was finally released in early 2009. This marked the longest gap in album releases for the band (four years). The album received decent reviews, but critics and fans were disappointed it wasn't as experimental as the band had originally promised—especially after the four years U2 spent working on it.

U2 360° Tour

To promote *No Line on the Horizon*, the band embarked on its U2 360° tour in mid-2009. The tour was U2's first venture with Live Nation, an American global entertainment company,

Atomic Bomb won nine Grammy Awards between 2005 and 2006.

ving Old Themes, Embracing New Technology, and Making History

When U2 formed, music was available on the radio and on vinyl records. They've seen the rise and fall of CDs, MTV, and VH1, and the advent of digital music files made available through platforms such as iTunes. In 2004, U2 partnered with Apple to cross-promote *Atomic Bomb* and a relatively new Apple gadget: the iPod. The U2 song "Vertigo" was used in Apple's iPod commercial. Unfortunately, modern technologies have also posed issues that didn't exist when U2 formed in 1976. For instance, when Edge's demo version of *Atomic Bomb* was stolen four months before the album was released, it was leaked online—including "Mercy," a song from the demo that wasn't on the final release. The song grew a big following online. The lyrics are in the booklet for the album's Special Limited Edition but it wasn't officially released until its inclusion on U2's *Wide Awake in Europe* vinyl-only live album in 2010.[4]

under a twelve-year, $100-million deal. Live Nation assumed control over U2's touring, merchandising, and official website.[5]

U2 360° was characterized by an "in the round" style with a circular stage, allowing the audience to encircle the band. This introduced the need for innovative concert structures

Rolling Stone hailed U2 as one of eight Artists of the Decade in 2009.[6]

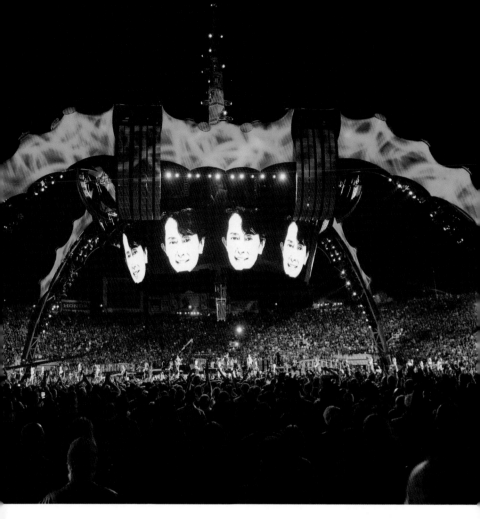

This October 2009 performance at the Rose Bowl in California demonstrates the "in the round" style U2 incorporated into their 360° Tour.

and techniques; at the time, the stage was the largest ever built. In October 2009, U2 set a US record for single concert attendance at the Rose Bowl in California (more than ninety-seven thousand people).[7] Despite a serious back injury Bono sustained, forcing U2 to reschedule notable performances such as the 2010 Glastonbury Festival and some of their North American appearances, the tour set records for the highest-grossing concert tour and highest-attended tour.

ving Old Themes, Embracing New Technology, and Making History

Churning into the 2010s

By 2010, the world's most successful band had been together for thirty-four years, its members approaching their fifties. Mullen's, Bono's, and Edge's children were grown or growing up, approaching the ages their parents were when they formed U2. Clayton, the band's long-standing bachelor, had his first child in 2010 (Clayton didn't wed until 2013, when he married human-rights lawyer Mariana Teixeira de Carvalho).[1]

All those years together as bandmates and friends, and still, U2 couldn't complete their next album to all the members' satisfaction.

Bidding Farewell to an Old Friend and Returning to Their Childhoods

In 2013, U2s long-time manager, Paul McGuinness, stepped down from his post. The band's first and only official manager, McGuinness began managing U2 in 1978. The band's Live Nation deal, signed in 2009, acquired McGuinness's management firm, but required him to resign. Guy Oseary, Madonna's manager, took over U2's management. McGuinness stuck by U2 through its many

Unable to determine the direction they wanted to go in for the next album, U2 focused on other major projects that spanned an array of sounds, methods, genres, and levels of contribution:

- A traditional rock album produced by Danger Mouse
- A dance-centric album produced by hip-hop artists RedOne and will.i.am
- A new song called "Ordinary Love" for the film *Mandela: Long Walk to Freedom*. The song was a tribute to Nelson Mandela and won the 2014 Golden Globe for Best Original Song.
- In 2014, another new song called "Invisible" debuted in a Super Bowl ad and was made available for free on iTunes to launch Product RED, an AIDS-fighting charitable effort.

Bono, of course, continued his political and charitable work while the band endeavored to find a path for their thirteenth album.

ups and downs, often advising them to stick to courses that supported their lofty principles. He made shrewd business decisions such as U2 3D concert films, U2-branded iPods, BlackBerry sponsorships, and the first-ever concert streamed live on YouTube.[2]

Pictured here immediately to the left of Bono, U2's manager of thirty-one years, Paul McGuinness, had to resign after U2 signed a deal with Live Nation in 2009.

After McGuinness's departure, U2 released their thirteenth studio album, *Songs of Innocence*, in September 2014, ending a five-and-a-half-year hiatus after 2009's *No Line on the Horizon*. *Songs of Innocence* explored the band members' childhoods in Ireland, including love and loss. Remarkably, despite the personal nature of *Achtung Baby* and a handful of other songs on the band's many albums, Bono called *Songs of Innocence* the band's most personal album to date.[3]

By the time *Songs of Innocence* was released, U2 had been together for thirty-eight years. According to Bono, the band

U2's togetherness is a testament to enduring bonds that began in adolescence.

wanted to be reminded of the things that originally inspired them to pursue music when they were teenagers in Dublin: "Let's try to figure out why we wanted to be in a band, the relationships around the band, our friendships, our lovers, our family. The whole album is first journeys—first journeys geographically, spiritually, sexually."[4]

Songs of Innocence sold only 101,000 copies in North America. It charted for only eight and nine weeks in the United States and United Kingdom, respectively, adding to the pain the controversial iTunes release caused. U2's status was further compromised by a serious bicycle accident Bono suffered in New York's Central Park in late 2014; he fractured his shoulder, humerus, and other bones, leading to doubts about his ability to perform on the subsequent Innocence + Experience tour.

Bono and U2 Revive

Following Bono's recovery, U2 went on the Innocence + Experience Tour in May 2015. The performances were thematic and autobiographical: innocence passing into experience, as demonstrated by the selected songs for each half (for the first time, U2 had an intermission in a concert). The set was impressive: the stage spanned the length of venue floors and had three sections, a connecting walkway, and a double-sided screen with an interior catwalk. The final date had to be rescheduled due to the November 13, 2015, terrorist attacks in Paris, but once rescheduled and performed, the tour's final performance in Paris was filmed for Innocence + Experience: Live in Paris video and broadcast on HBO.

Churning into the 2010s

In September 2014, U2 announced they were releasing their thirteenth album, *Songs of Innocence*. This was an Apple product launch event, released digitally to all iTunes customers for free. Apple paid Universal Music Group and U2 a lump sum of money for a five-week period of distribution exclusivity and spent $100 million on a promo campaign. The release met with a huge backlash. Apple had directly installed the album into the library of five hundred million iTunes users, many of whom were furious to find the album installed without their permission—even for free. U2 agreed to the promo over fears that the "paying public's appetite for further releases was in terminal decline,"[5] a fear of many bands as the traditional music industry continues to decline. Apple had to release a tool to remove the album from customers' accounts, and both Apple and U2 continue to receive criticism for overstepping.

A companion album to *Songs of Innocence*, *Songs of Experience*, was planned for a 2016 release. However, U2 wasn't done making political statements: in a return to old-school U2 values, the band delayed the *Songs of Experience* release due to a conservative-leaning shift in global politics, notably the Brexit decision in the United Kingdom and the 2016 presidential election of Donald Trump. Although *Songs of Experience* was mostly completed by the end of 2016, U2 chose to reasses the album's tone so they could write lyrics and music more reflective of the times. While reevaluating *Songs of Experience*'s place on the global stage, U2 embarked on a thirtieth-anniversary *Joshua Tree* tour, performing the album in its entirety at each show. The anniversary *Joshua*

U2 performs at New York's Madison Square Garden in July 2015 on their Innocence + Experience Tour.

Forty-one years after forming, U2 poses at the 2017 MAP Fund Benefit Concert honoring U2 bassist Adam Clayton. They've weathered decades of ups and downs to become musical legends.

Tree tour was the first U2 tour promoting an old album rather than a new release. The Edge said the same world events that delayed *Songs of Experience* inspired the group to retour with *Joshua Tree*, which contained relevant sociopolitical themes.[6]

In December 2017, *Songs of Experience* finally released. The album is a collection of letters written by Bono to the people and places he holds most dear, inspired by his grave bicycle accident a couple years before. Many of the lyrics were rewritten to reflect dissatisfaction with the political climate.

To avoid the controversy spurred by the iTunes release of its predecessor, *Songs of Innocence*, *Songs of Experience* was subtly promoted: U2 sent postal letters to fans to tease the album's release.[7] Though received with mixed reviews, *Songs*

Bono's son Eli and Edge's daughter Sian are holding hands on the cover of *Songs of Experience.*

of Experience still debuted at number one in the United States, making U2 the first-ever band to top US charts for four consecutive decades.

All That They've Seen

U2 has been together for more than forty years. Despite several low points that threatened the band's unity, the original four have all remained. Unlike many of their peers in the music business, who have disbanded or lost members to illnesses, addictions, or age, U2 remains steadfast. They never seem to slow down, not musically or politically.

U2 has witnessed a great many things in their more than four decades together—four decades they did not witness passively. When they saw something wrong, they wrote and sang about it. They campaigned against it. They raised funds to fight it.

The story of U2 is one of perseverance, friendship, and a unity forged in the fire of a greater purpose. The band's commitment to pretty much everything but financial gain has united them. (In fact, they didn't really begin to see profits from their albums or concerts until the early 1990s; they spent much of their early money just trying to innovate and on making personal connections with fans). They've taken breaks to nurture their friendships and togetherness.

With such a winning approach, who knows what the future still holds for the scrappy little band with heavy hearts and poignant principles from a divided Dublin and strife-ridden Ireland.

Timeline

1960 Adam Clayton is born on March 13 in Chinnor, England; Paul David Hewson, aka "Bono," is born on May 10 in Dublin, Ireland.

1961 David Howell Evans, aka "the Edge," is born on August 8 in East London, England; Larry Mullen Jr. is born on October 31 in Artane (Dublin), Ireland.

1974 Bono's mother dies of an aneurysm after her father's funeral in September.

1976 U2 is founded in Larry Mullen's kitchen on September 25 under the name Larry Mullen Band, which quickly is renamed Feedback; Larry Mullen's mother dies in a car accident.

1978 The band wins a contest in Limerick that awards them £500 in prize money and studio time to record their first demo; Paul McGuinness becomes the band's manager.

1979 Their first release is an Irish-only single called "U2:3" in September, which tops Irish national charts; in December, U2 goes to London to perform their first shows outside of Ireland.

1980 U2 releases a second Irish-only single called "Another Day" on February 26; Island Records signs U2 to their first international contract in March; their first international single "11 O'Clock Tick Tock" is released in May and fails to chart; *Boy*, U2's first album, is released in October.

1981 In March, Bono loses lyric and music ideas backstage during a nightclub performance in Portland; U2 opens for Thin Lizzy at the Slane Concert in August, which the Edge calls one of the worst shows the band ever played; *October*, U2's second album, is released in October.

1983 In January, the single "New Year's Day" is released and becomes the band's first hit outside Ireland or the United Kingdom; *War*, U2's third album, is released in February; Red Rocks concert on June 5 is hailed as one of "50 Moments that Changed the History of Rock and Roll" by *Rolling Stone*.

1984 *The Unforgettable Fire*, U2's fourth album, is released in October.

1985 U2 plays at the iconic Live Aid concert at London's Wembley Stadium.

1986 U2 joins the Conspiracy of Hope tour, benefiting Amnesty International.

1987 *The Joshua Tree*, U2's hugely successful fifth album, is released in March; "With or Without You" becomes the band's first number one single in the United States; U2 performs on the roof of a shop in downtown Los Angeles on March 27 to film the video for "Where the Streets Have No Name."

1988 *Rattle and Hum*, U2's sixth album release, is a double album.

1989 U2 embarks on the Lovetown tour to promote the album *Rattle and Hum* but only brings the tour to Australasia, Japan, and Europe; Clayton is arrested for marijuana possession.

1990 U2 begins work on their seventh album, *Achtung Baby*, at Berlin's Hansa Studios in October.

1991 U2 returns to Dublin to finish *Achtung Baby*, which is released in November.

1993 *Achtung Baby* produces five hit singles and wins a Grammy; U2 signs a six-album deal to stay with Island Records/PolyGram and releases the *Zooropa* album in July.

1994 *Zooropa,* U2's eighth album, wins the Grammy for Best Alternative Music Album.

1995 In June, U2 releases a chart-topping single on the *Batman Forever* soundtrack titled "Hold Me, Thrill Me, Kiss Me, Kill Me"; U2 begins recording their ninth album *Pop.*

1997 In September, U2 is the first band to play in Sarajevo following the Bosnian War.

1998 U2 releases the compilation *The Best of 1980–1990,* which enjoys the highest first-week sales of any greatest-hits record in the United States; U2 begins recording their tenth album, *All That You Can't Leave Behind.*

2000 *All That You Can't Leave Behind* is released in October and debuts at number one in thirty-two countries.

2001 The song "Beautiful Day" wins a Grammy for Song of the Year, Best Rock Performance by a Duo or Group with Vocal, and Record of the Year; U2 embarks on the Elevation tour.

2002 "Walk On" wins the Grammy for Record of the Year and is the first time an artist won this award in consecutive years for songs from one album; U2 releases its second compilation *The Best of 1990–2000.*

2004 *How to Dismantle an Atomic Bomb,* U2's eleventh album, is released in November and is number one in thirty countries.

2005 In March, U2 is inducted into the Rock and Roll Hall of Fame by Bruce Springsteen in their first year of induction eligibility.

2006 In September, U2 plays at the Louisiana Superdome in New Orleans prior to the Saints' first home game since Hurricane Katrina; U2 begins recording their twelfth album *No Line on the Horizon.*

2009 U2 sets a US record for single concert attendance at the Rose Bowl in California (more than ninety-seven thousand people).

2013 Paul McGuinness, who managed U2 for more than thirty years, steps down.

2014 A new song called "Invisible" debuts in a Super Bowl ad and is made available for free on iTunes to launch Product Red, an AIDS-fighting charitable effort; in September, U2 announces they are releasing their thirteenth album *Songs of Innocence*; Bono has a bicycle accident in New York's Central Park and fractures his shoulder, humerus, and other bones.

2015 Following Bono's recovery, U2 goes on the Innocence + Experience tour in May.

2017 U2's fourteenth album *Songs of Experience* is released in December and debuts at number one in the United States, making U2 the first-ever band to top US charts in four consecutive decades.

Discography

1980 *Boy*

1981 *October*

1983 *War*
Under a Blood Red Sky

1984 *The Unforgettable Fire*

1987 *The Joshua Tree*

1988 *Rattle and Hum*

1991 *Achtung Baby*

1993 *Zooropa*

1997 *Pop*

1998 *The Best of 1980–1990 & B-Sides*
The Best of 1980–1990

2000 *All That You Can't Leave Behind*

2002 *The Best of 1990–2000 & B-Sides*
The Best of 1990–2000

2004 *How to Dismantle an Atomic Bomb*

2006 *18 Singles*

2007 *The Joshua Tree 20th Anniversary Edition*

2008 *Boy (Remastered)*
October (Remastered)
War (Remastered)
Under a Blood Red Sky (Remastered)

2009 *The Unforgettable Fire (Remastered)*
No Line on the Horizon

2014 *Songs of Innocence*

2017 *Songs of Experience*

Chapter Notes

Introduction

1. Fuzz97, "U2 Sunday Bloody Sunday Live from Slane Castle," YouTube, May 4, 2007, https://www.youtube.com/watch?v=gbNuIqiVPbU.
2. "Omagh Bombing," *Britannica Library*, April 13, 2017, library.eb.com/levels/referencecenter/article/Omagh-bombing/603841.
3. Joe Marvilli, "Rock History 101: U2's 'Sunday Bloody Sunday,'" ConsequenceofSound.net, November 7, 2009, https://consequenceofsound.net/2009/11/rock-history-101-u2s-sunday-bloody-sunday/.
4. "Bloody Sunday," *Britannica Library*, September 22, 2011, library.eb.com/levels/referencecenter/article/Bloody-Sunday/389458.
5. "@U2's Awards & Recognition," atU2.com, https://www.atu2.com/about/awards (accessed March 16, 2018).

1
From Schoolmates to Bandmates

1. U2 and Neil McCormick, *U2 by U2* (New York, N.Y.: Dey Street Books, 2009), p. 34.
2. John Jobling, *U2: The Definitive Biography* (New York, N.Y.: St. Martin's Griffin, 2015), p. 3.
3. U2 and McCormick, p. 31.
4. "History," Mount Temple Comprehensive, http://www.mounttemple.ie/about-mount-temple/history/ (accessed March 16, 2018).
5. "Northern Ireland Troubles," *World History: The Modern Era*, ABC-CLIO, 2018, https://worldhistory.abc-clio.com/Search/Display/309851 (accessed March 8, 2018).
6. U2 and McCormick, p. 9.
7. Ibid., p. 351.

8. "Larry Mullen's Biography," Three Chords and the Truth, http://www.threechordsandthetruth.net/u2bios/u2larrybio.php (accessed March 16, 2018).
9. "Larry Mullen Jr. Biography," atU2.com, https://www.atu2.com/band/larry (accessed March 16, 2018).
10. "100 Greatest Drummers of All Time," *Rolling Stone,* March 31, 2016, https://www.rollingstone.com/music/lists/100-greatest-drummers-of-all-time-20160331/larry-mullen-jr-20160329.
11. U2 and McCormick, p. 317.
12. Ibid., p. 55.
13. Lisa Robinson, "U2's Unforgettable Fire," *Vanity Fair*, February 18, 2014, https://www.vanityfair.com/culture/2004/11/u2-success-story.
14. U2 and McCormick, pp. 150–152.
15. "100 Greatest Guitarists," *Rolling Stone*, December 18, 2015, https://www.rollingstone.com/music/lists/100-greatest-guitarists-20111123/the-edge-20111122.

2
The Early Years

1. "U2 History," atU2.com, https://www.atu2.com/band (accessed March 16, 2018).
2. John Jobling, *U2: The Definitive Biography* (New York, N.Y.: St. Martin's Griffin, 2015), p. 27.
3. Ibid., p. 22.
4. JT Griffith, "AllMusic Review by JT Griffith," AllMusic, https://www.allmusic.com/album/u2-three-single-mw0001186799 (accessed March 16, 2018).
5. James Henke, "Blessed Are the Peacemakers, U2," *Rolling Stone,* June 9, 1983, https://www.rollingstone.com/music/features/blessed-are-the-peacemakers-19830609.
6. "Bono Speaks," *U2 Magazine*, February 10, 1984.

3
Fate, Faith, "Fire," and Flags

1. "Fire/R.O.K.," U2 Songs, http://www.u2songs.com/discography/u2_fire_r.o.k._single (accessed March 16, 2018).
2. "Republican Hunger Strikes in the Maze Prison," BBC, http://www.bbc.co.uk/history/events/republican_hunger_strikes_maze (accessed March 16, 2018).
3. Ger Siggins, "Flashback 1981...Thin Lizzy Headline Slane," *Independent*, August 16, 2015, https://www.independent.ie/life/flashback-1981-thin-lizzy-headline-slane-31446407.html.
4. Joseph Rose, "How U2, a Portland Bar and a Missing Briefcase Altered Music History," *Oregonian*, April 28, 2016, http://www.oregonlive.com/history/2016/03/u2_portland_stolen_briefcase_h.html.
5. U2 and Neil McCormick, *U2 by U2* (New York, N.Y.: Dey Street Books, 2009).
6. "100 Best Albums of the Eighties," *Rolling Stone*, November 16, 1989, https://www.rollingstone.com/music/lists/100-best-albums-of-the-eighties-20110418/u2-war-20110322.
7. Simon Reynolds, *Rip It Up and Start Again: Postpunk 1978–1984* (New York, N.Y.: Penguin Books, 2006).
8. "50 Moments That Changed the History of Rock and Roll," *Rolling Stone*, June 24, 2004, https://www.rollingstone.com/music/news/50-moments-that-changed-rock-and-roll-otis-and-jimi-burn-it-up-20040624.

4
Jumping into the Fire

1. Christopher Connelly, "U2: Keeping the Faith," *Rolling Stone*, March 14, 1985, https://www.rollingstone.com/music/features/keeping-the-faith-19850314.

2. Kurt Loder, "The Unforgettable Fire," *Rolling Stone*, October 11, 1984, https://www.rollingstone.com/music/albumreviews/the-unforgettable-fire-19841011.
3. Robert Christgau, "Christgau's Consumer Guide," *Village Voice*, February 5, 1985, https://www.robertchristgau.com/xg/cg/cgv2-85.php.
4. Connelly.
5. Ibid.
6. Gavin Edwards, "U2's 'Bad' Break: 12 Minutes at Live Aid That Made the Band's Career," *Rolling Stone*, July 10, 2014, https://www.rollingstone.com/music/artists/u2/biography.
7. Andy Greene, "How Amnesty International Rocked the World: The Inside Story, *Rolling Stone*, October 25, 2013, https://www.rollingstone.com/music/news/how-amnesty-international-rocked-the-world-the-inside-story-20131025.

5
Crossing the Desert Ends in Rattled Nerves

1. Paul Grein, "Silver, Platinum, and Gold: A Chart History of U2's 'The Joshua Tree," Yahoo! Music, March 6, 2017, https://www.yahoo.com/music/silver-platinum-and-gold-a-chart-history-of-u2s-the-joshua-tree-222843507.html.
2. "El Salvadoran Civil War," *World History: The Modern Era*, ABC-CLIO, 2018, worldhistory.abc-clio.com/Search/Display/309668.
3. Jane Rodgers, "Joshua Trees," National Park Service, updated March 21, 2016, https://www.nps.gov/jotr/learn/nature/jtrees.htm.
4. Don McLeese, "The Pride and Passion of U2," *Chicago Sun-Times*, April 12, 1987, https://www.atu2.com/news/the-pride-and-passion-of-u2.html.
5. Dean Van Nguyen, "Where the Streets Have No Statues: Why Do the Irish Hate U2?" *Guardian*, July 12, 2017, https://www.

theguardian.com/music/2017/jul/12/where-the-streets-have-no-statues-why-do-the-irish-hate-u2.

6. Elysa Gardner, "Achtung, Baby," *Rolling Stone*, January 9, 1992, https://www.rollingstone.com/music/albumreviews/achtung-baby-19920109.

7. Jon Pareles, "RECORDINGS; When Self-Importance Interferes with the Music," *New York Times*, October 16, 1988, http://www.nytimes.com/1988/10/16/arts/recordings-when-self-importance-interferes-with-the-music.html.

8. Anthony Curtis, "U2's Edge and Adam Clayton Look Back on Two Decades of Hit Albums with Few—if Any—Regrets," *Revolver*, December 1, 2000, https://www.atu2.com/news/u2s-edge-and-adam-clayton-look-back-on-two-decades-of-hit-albums-with-few-if-any-regrets.html.

9. Sam Adams, David Fear, Tim Grierson, Kory Grow, Eric Hynes, and Jason Neman, "40 Greatest Rock Documentaries," *Rolling Stone*, August 15, 2014, https://www.rollingstone.com/movies/lists/40-greatest-rock-documentaries-20140815/u2-rattle-and-hum-1988-20140815.

10. Bono, "Dream It All Up Again," atU2.com, December 30, 1989, https://www.atu2.com/news/dream-it-all-up-again.html

6
Returning to Their Roots: Geopolitical Reunification Revives U2

1. "Berlin Wall," History.com, 2009, http://www.history.com/topics/cold-war/berlin-wall.

2. Bill Flanagan, *U2 At The End of The World* (New York, NY: Delacorte Press, 1995), pp. 1–4.

3. Matt McGee, "U2's History, atU2.com, https://www.atu2.com/band/bio.html (accessed March 16, 2018).

4. Anthony DeCurtis, "Zoo World Order," *Rolling Stone*, October 14, 1993, https://www.rollingstone.com/music/features/zoo-world-order-19931014.

5. "U2 Zoo TV Tour," U2gigs.com, http://www.u2gigs.com/show946.html (accessed March 16, 2018).

7
Speeding Toward the Millennium and Beyond

1. "Bosnia and Herzegovina," *Britannica Library*, December 6, 2017, library.eb.com/levels/referencecenter/article/Bosnia-and-Herzegovina/110558.
2. Aida Cerkez, "Bosnia Joins Rockers U2 in the Name of Love Sarajevo Concert Brings Warring Factions Together," *Spokesman–Review*, September 24, 1997, http://www.spokesman.com/stories/1997/sep/24/bosnia-joins-rockers-u2-in-the-name-of-love/.
3. "Stuck in a Moment: 9/11 and U2," *Daily Record*, September 11, 2009, https://joelfrancis.com/2009/09/11/stuck-in-a-moment-911-and-u2.
4. Dan Hanzus, "Why U2's Super Bowl Halftime Show Was the Greatest," NFL.com, November 30, 2017, www.nfl.com/news/story/0ap3000000885742/article/why-u2s-super-bowl-halftime-show-was-the-greatest.
5. Phil Gallo, "The Grammys: U2 and Sharp Keys; Soul Star, Bono Tops with 'O'bro,'" *Variety*, February 28, 2002, https://www.highbeam.com/doc/1G1-84052164.html.

8
Reviving Old Themes, Embracing New Technology, and Making History

1. "U2 and 3 Songs," documentary within the DVD packaged with *How to Dismantle an Atomic Bomb* album.
2. Andy Greene, "20 Insanely Great U2 Songs Only Hardcore Fans Know," *Rolling Stone*, March 14, 2014, https://www.rollingstone.com/music/pictures/20-insanely-great-u2-songs-only-hardcore-fans-know-20140314/19-mercy-0189045.

3. Alex Rawls, "'A Beautiful Day': When U2, Green Day Reopened the Superdome," MySpiltMilk.com, NOLA.com, October 31, 2016, http://www.nola.com/music/index.ssf/2016/09/10_years_after_the_domecoming.html.

4. Jon Pareles, "Last Gang in Town," *New York Times*, March 2, 2009, https://www.nytimes.com/2009/03/01/arts/music/01Pare.html.

5. Ray Waddell, "U2 Signs 12-Year Deal with Live Nation," *Billboard*, March 31, 2008, https://www.billboard.com/articles/news/1046023/u2-signs-12-year-deal-with-live-nation.

6. "Best of The Decade," *Rolling Stone*, December 9, 2009, https://www.rollingstone.com/music/news/the-2000s-best-of-the-decade-the-new-issue-of-rolling-stone-20091209.

7. "Rose Bowl Concert on DVD," U2.com, http://www.u2.com/news/title/rose-bowl-concert-on-dvd/

9
Churning into the 2010s

1. Ken Sweeney, "Adam Clayton Weds His Brazilian Girlfriend in Dublin Sunshine," *Independent*, September 4, 2013, https://www.independent.ie/woman/celeb-news/adam-clayton-weds-his-brazilian-girlfriend-in-dublin-sunshine-29551509.html.

2. Andrew Edgecliff-Johnson, "Lunch with the FT: Paul McGuinness," FT.com, December 4, 2009, https://www.ft.com/content/8c1788d2-e059-11de-8494-00144feab49a.

3. "New U2 Album Given Away for Free to iTunes Users," BBC News, September 9, 2014, http://www.bbc.com/news/entertainment-arts-29132508.

4. "Exclusive: Bono Reveals Secrets of U2's Surprise Album 'Songs of Innocence,'" *Rolling Stone*, September 9, 2014, https://www.rollingstone.com/music/news/u2-surprise-album-songs-of-innocence-apple-itunes-free-20140909.

5. Adam Sherwin, "Free U2 Album: How the Most Generous Giveaway in Music History Turned PR Disaster," *Independent*,

September 19, 2014, https://www.independent.co.uk/arts-entertainment/music/features/free-u2-album-how-the-most-generous-giveaway-in-music-history-turned-into-a-pr-disaster-9745028.html.

6. Jon Pareles, "Review: U2 Revisits 'The Joshua Tree' in the Here and Now," *New York Times*, May 15, 2017, https://www.nytimes.com/2017/05/15/arts/music/u2-joshua-tree-30th-anniversary-tour-review.html.

7. Ashley Iasimone, "U2 Fans Receive Mysterious 'Blackout' Letters," *Billboard*, August 21, 2017, https://www.billboard.com/articles/columns/rock/7934336/u2-fans-receive-mysterious-blackout-letters.

Glossary

Anglican A type of Protestant religion with ties to the Church of England.

arena rock Popularized in the 1970s, this type of rock music is recorded and produced with large audiences in mind. Also known as stadium rock, this type of music is usually highly produced and radio-friendly, and can be upbeat as well as somber and balladic. Arena rock music usually has an anthemic sound and effect, meaning it includes notable lyrics intended to loop in listeners and audience members; a popular example is "We Will Rock You" by the band Queen.

Cold War Political hostilities between Soviet bloc nations (the USSR) and the Western world, specifically the United States, that lasted from 1945 (the end of World War II) to 1990 (the fall of the Soviet Union).

German reunification In 1990, the political, social, and economic reunification of the Federal Republic of Germany (West Germany) and the Communist German Democratic Republic (East Germany) into one united German nation following the disintegration of the Communist Soviet Union, to which East Germany had been loyal since 1949. The term also refers to the reunification of East and West Berlin; the German capital city had been divided by the Berlin Wall since 1961.

gold album/record An album that sells a minimum of 500,000 copies (albums can include singles or full-length albums).

IRA (Irish Republican Army) Any paramilitary (unofficial military force) movements in Ireland during the twentieth and twenty-first centuries that were devoted to Irish republicanism—the notion that all of Ireland, including Northern Ireland (which has remained a part of the United Kingdom), should be one unified, independent republic.

philanthropy An initiative or act done for humanitarian purposes (to better human life).

platinum album A music album that has sold a minimum of one million copies.

pop music A type of popular music that is typically characterized by traits that appeal to a wide, general audience rather than appealing to a specific demographic or to express a specific ideology.

post-punk A type of rock music inspired by punk but typically less aggressive and more experimental than punk.

punk music A kind of rock music popular in the late 1970s known for its loud, incessant sound and often aggressive lyrics. Punk rockers and their fans often adopted extreme forms of dress and style, as well as behavior intended to defy societal norms.

sociopolitical Of, relating to, or involving a combination of social and political factors.

surrealist Describes artists or writers who adhere to new and unusual or experimental ideas, often with the purpose of releasing creativity

synthesizer An electronic instrument that, especially in the 1970s and 1980s, became popular in the production of music. Synthesizers convert sound through other musical instruments, such as amplifiers or speakers, and can imitate other musical sounds, such as the piano, the flute, and even vocals.

synthpop A type of music that became popular in the late 1970s and into the 1980s that relies heavily on the synthesizer to create the dominant sound and backbone of a musical track.

The Troubles A period of violence and terrorist activity between Irish Republic loyalists, who were usually Roman Catholic, and United Kingdom loyalists, who were usually Protestant, in Ireland, especially Northern Ireland, that lasted thirty years (1968–1998).

Further Reading

Books

50MINUTES.com. *Bloody Sunday: The Bogside Massacre*. Brussels, Belgium: Plurilingua Publishing, 2017.

Jobling, John. *U2: The Definitive Biography*. New York, NY: Thomas Dunne Books, 2014.

Kamberg, Mary-Lane. *Bono: Fighting World Hunger and Poverty*. New York, NY: Rosen Publishing, 2008.

Pollack, Pam, and Meg Belviso. *Who Is Bono?* New York, NY: Penguin Workshop, 2018.

Smyth, Jim. *Remembering the Troubles: Contesting the Recent Past in Northern Ireland*. Notre Dame, IN: University of Notre Dame Press, 2017.

Stokes, Niall, and Brian Boyd. *U2: Songs + Experience*. London, England: Carlton Books, 2018.

Trachtenberg, Martha P. *Bono: Rock Star Activist*. Berkeley Heights, NJ: Enslow Publishers, 2008.

U2 and Neil McCormick. *U2 by U2*. New York, NY: Dey Street Books, 2009.

Websites

@U2

www.AtU2.com

Operated for more than twenty years by U2 fans for U2 fans, this site includes bios, lyrics, photos, and U2 news.

ONE

www.one.org

The official site of ONE, a campaigning and advocacy organization of more than nine million people acting to end extreme poverty and preventable disease.

U2.com

www.U2.com

The official site of U2, U2.com gives visitors access to news, photos, merchandise, tour information, and a special page called "Hearts + Minds," which details the band's collaborations and campaigns to make the world a better place.

Films

From the Sky Down (2011), directed by Davis Guggenheim.

U2 at the BBC: Special Edition (2017), http://www.bbc.co.uk/ programmes/b09m6cdj.

Index

punk rock, 40

R

Rattle and Hum, 57–59, 68
religion
  band's faith and spirituality, 18,
    21, 25, 38, 44, 55
  conflict between Catholics and
    Protestants, 11–12, 19
Republic of Ireland, 11–12,
  19, 37–38, 56
Rock and Roll Hall of
  Fame, 7, 78–79
Rolling Stone
  accolades from, 7, 16, 25, 40–43,
    44, 50–51, 52, 59, 72, 79, 82
  interviews with, 40, 49
  reviews by, 47, 57, 59

S

Sarajevo, 67, 71–72
Self Aid, 56
September 11 attacks, 75
Slane Castle, 5, 37–39, 46
Songs of Experience, 89–91
Songs of Innocence, 86–88
spirituality and faith, 18, 21, 25,
  38, 44, 55
"Sunday Bloody Sunday," 5–7, 13,
  40–41, 49, 56
Super Bowl, 75–76, 85
synthesizers, 30, 40

T

360° Tour, 81–83
the Troubles, 6, 10–13, 19, 40, 56

U

U2
  in the 1970s and 1980s, 8–25,
    26–33, 34–43, 44–51, 52–59
  in the 1990s, 60–68, 69–71
  in the 2000s and 2010s, 5, 72–76,
    77–83, 84–91
  awards and honors received,
    7, 53, 54, 67–68, 72,
    76, 78–79, 81
  band members'
    backgrounds, 8–25
  dislike of, 56, 74
  faith and spirituality of, 18, 21,
    25, 38, 44, 55
  in iTunes controversy, 87–88, 90
  lyrical themes of, 24, 31–33, 40,
    53–57, 63, 77–79, 87
  philanthropic work by, 7, 21, 25,
    51, 52, 56, 71–74, 80, 85
  as political band, 5–7, 21–22,
    24, 40–41, 46, 56, 60–
    67, 75, 89–90
  Rolling Stone rankings of, 7,
    16, 25, 40–43, 51, 52, 59,
    72, 79, 82
The Unforgettable Fire, 45–47, 52

W

War (album), 5–6, 21, 39–43, 44, 46
"Where the Streets Have No
  Name," 53–56
"With or Without You," 54, 56–57

Z

Zooropa, 67–68
Zoo TV tour, 66–68